COLLEGE
WITHOUT THE
CAMPUS

COLLEGE
WITHOUT THE
CAMPUS

HILLARY HARSHMAN

LEANING LINDEN BOOKS

Published by Leaning Linden Books.
Walla Walla, Washington
leaninglindenbooks@gmail.com

ISBN 978-0-9973080-0-6 (paperback)
ISBN 978-0-9973080-1-3 (hardcover)
ISBN 978-0-9973080-2-0 (e-book)

Copy editor: Nancy Halseide
Cover design: Micah Kandros
Interior design: Stewart A. Williams
Indexing: Laura Shelley

Library of Congress Control Number: 2016909061

Printed in the United States of America.

CONTENTS

To my grandparents for their support and encouragement

INTRODUCTION

Attending college had been a goal of mine since before middle school. I can remember being asked by peers and friends if I intended to go to college, and I remember responding affirmatively, thinking to myself that of course I would continue my education after high school—that's just what dedicated students did. As a young student, I wasn't fully aware of the cost of college, but I knew that college was held in esteem by my family and friends and that it led to influential life opportunities. The positivity I associated with college removed the accompanying expenses from the forefront of my mind.

But by high school, my awareness of money had become acute. I would soon be spending the average price of $14,262 per year at a public four-year school or $33,804 per year at a private nonprofit four-year school.[1] To add to my monetary trepidation, my new awareness wasn't just about cost. Leaving home, getting a job, and paying for college all became necessary issues for me to consider.

It was in my second year of high school that a friend loaned my family *Accelerated Distance Learning*, an instructive guide that would change my life. Author Brad Voeller shares tools and methods to earn a fully-accredited degree using distance learning techniques to save both time and money. His book became my key resource for the next six years, guiding my selection of a college, informing me of various credit-earning methods to expand my pool of resources, and encouraging me to complete my degree goals.

As I began to earn my degree by putting Brad Voeller's advice into action, I needed to explain to others what I was doing and why. Though my immediate family had researched these distance-learning methods along with me and knew what I was doing, other family and friends unfamiliar with off-campus learning were reasonably skeptical of my decisions, probing me about worries of, "Will your degree be legitimate?" "What about the college experience?" and "How are you going to meet people if you aren't on campus?"

Since these were questions I too wanted answered, I researched off-campus college so I was confident that distance learning could allow me to achieve quality education faster and without debt. I didn't plan to complete my whole degree off campus; instead, I committed to one year of off-campus study, knowing that if this method didn't suit me, I could take a different path the following year. I began to tell others about the new subjects I was learning and the tests I was taking, and this helped them see the feasibility of my decision.

Since year one of college without the campus went well, I began year two in the same manner. The information became more advanced, but I was motivated and excited by this style of learning. Two years became three, and then I was a senior. My final year was different from the rest, as I selected a college and enrolled. This year was my hardest, but I studied and tested until all my degree requirements were complete. I had finished!

Graduating from college was surreal. I could hardly believe that I had achieved the goal I had worked toward for over four years—now I was a bachelor's degree holder. What would this mean for me and how would it affect what came next in my life?

As with any change, I had feelings of both confidence and uncertainty regarding my future and past. Part of my confidence about the past came from the fact that I had earned my degree economically without skimping on quality. While my upbringing included thriftiness and budgeting, it wasn't until high school that I thought to apply frugality to college. This thriftiness played a huge part in my feeling of success at the finish line.

I was also grateful for the four years of closeness with my family—not only with my parents and my sister, but with my four grandparents, aunts, uncles, and cousins. I realize that having the opportunity for strong familial connection is not to be taken lightly, and I am thankful that I could use the flexibility of my school schedule to learn from and be there for my family in an ongoing fashion, especially during the crucial young adult stage.

As for uncertainty, I inwardly wrestled with thoughts that my college experience had been too cheap to actually be valid. Many of my initial doubts came back to haunt me. How did I explain to others that the school I chose was legitimate? Simply stating, "I graduated from Thomas Edison State University in New Jersey," followed by "But I never had to go there," was a surefire way to raise some red flags. I was thrilled that I had saved a substantial amount of money, but instead of eagerly compiling a final total of my expenses, I was reluctant to total my college costs for fear I had exceeded my tentative goal of $10,000.

Writing this book proved excellent for resolving these doubts. I dived into the world of accreditation, equipping myself with data and facts to understand how to tell between scam and sound colleges. I rehashed my strenuous senior year of upper-level credits. I even calculated my expenses.

Now I organize my findings for you to use in combating the doubts and questions you may encounter.

USE MY STORY TO REACH YOUR GOALS

Explaining credit-by-exam testing and sharing my experience with this method is at the heart of why I decided to write this book. Even though I had confidence in my college decisions, it was nonetheless difficult at times to take a path quite different from that of my friends, which involved choosing to live at home to study, to not enroll until my senior year, and to test out of nearly all my classes. The most difficult part was not being 100 percent sure about the outcome of what I was doing. How helpful it would have been if I could have known at the beginning what I know now! Thus, this book exists to be an encouragement, a demystifier, and a resource for others completing their own degree.

College Without the Campus starts with the end of my college journey and works backwards to the beginning. I did this because I want to show the results of credit-by-exam testing first and later share the information you need to get started with this learning method. However, once you reach chapter 5, you may wish to read the remaining chapters in the order that they pertain to your goals. In chapter 14, you'll find a frequently asked question section, with the questions organized to correspond to the book's chapters. The FAQ section tackles a few of the nitty-gritty details of distance learning.

Through my college journey, I acquired knowledge, resilience, persistence, and individuality. I met new people, gained experience doing something unusual, and broadened my life experience. College was not just earning a degree; it was a voyage that I concluded debt-free, safe, enriched, and as the owner of my own fledgling business. Here's how you can sail closer to your educational dreams with less money and stress and more flexibility and customization.

CHAPTER 1

WHY COLLEGE?

If your experience is anything like mine, going to college has been something you've thought, heard, and studied about for a good portion of your life. Our society places substantial importance on earning a degree. Why is college good for a person? Let's address what compensation college graduates receive from their journey to a diploma and how achieving that degree off campus significantly sweetens the deal.

COLLEGE: A TIME FOR GROWTH

One of the best assets of college is the opportunity for growth. Many students entering the college scene have reached a point in their lives where they have more time and perhaps more money to allocate as they choose, and they are directing those resources toward learning. What is learned in college can help the student get a job, reach a promotion, or start down an entirely new path in life. A free-elective class may strike a chord and open the door to personal discovery.

For me, a bachelor's degree equaled four years of concentrated learning and self-improvement. It prevented me from becoming stale after high school and gave me time to address the many topics I wished to study at the college level, such as history, psychology, and mathematics.

With a bachelor's degree, a person can continue onto graduate studies which will give him a platform for accessing deeper research and new fields of study that were not open to him before. Completing this single achievement gives so many options! Educational goals now available are a master's degree, a professional degree, or a doctorate. The bachelor's degree is a basic stepping stone for numerous degree fields and occupations.

The same can be said for an associate degree. This degree adds depth to your résumé and shows that you took time to further your education after high school. It can also facilitate in transferring credit to a different field of study or from one school to another.

Of course, a major gain for those with a degree is the augmentation of the pool of jobs available. The graduate's possible job market has expanded to include not only jobs where no degree is needed but also jobs where an associate/bachelor's degree is required.

Additionally, the college grad has gained the potential to make more money over his lifetime. In 2013, people in the United States between the ages of 25 and 34 with a high school diploma or equivalent working full time earned an average of $30,000 per year while those with a bachelor's degree earned an average of $48,530.[2] That's a 62% increase! If we look at all U.S. citizens age 25 and older, those with a bachelor's degree earned on average $20,000 more each year than those who had a high school diploma or a GED certificate.[3]

COLLEGE COSTS

So why doesn't everyone get a bachelor's degree? The two simplest reasons are time and money. Not everyone has four or more years to devote to schooling after finishing high school. And certainly, not everyone can afford the increasing tuition. The average cost of one year of tuition plus room and board at public institutions in 2011-2012 was 39 percent higher than the cost of tuition, room, and board in 2001-2002, even after being adjusted for inflation.[4]

Abundant grants, loans, and scholarships available to students have helped counter these rising costs, yet there are still out-of-pocket expenses integral to college learning. It can be difficult to save this money before leaving for college, increasing the need to borrow money. A student may work while going to school to avoid borrowing, but there is a point where the amount of time spent working to pay off debt quicker negatively affects the quality of the education the debt is paying for.[5]

Then there is the effect college has on lifestyle. While many people have expressed to me their feelings that the campus experience is an important, even mandatory, part of life, others tell of their mixed experiences with regret as the negative friends, situations, and environment outweighed the positive aspects of college.

Now imagine that you could get a bachelor's degree in two years rather than four. Or, that you could study for six months of the year and take a study vacation during the other six. Imagine stretching out your degree without paying continuous tuition. How about being able to choose and modify your environment for learning and living? Attending college off campus offers all of this and a myriad of other alternatives matched to your current income, available time, and lifestyle.

Opportunity Cost

This leads us to a discussion of opportunity cost. This concept easily applies to students using their time and money to achieve a degree. The resources spent on their degree become unavailable for other expenditures, including property investments, savings, vehicle purchases, business endeavors, and time in relationships. The only reason we give up the opportunity to do these other things is that we believe our college education will provide the greatest return on our time and money. Through off-campus education, students can limit opportunity costs throughout their degree, using techniques such as studying on a punctuated or faster schedule and postponing enrollment until the college's services are needed, which will be discussed in chapter 3.

OFF-CAMPUS HURDLES

Say you are a person who has decided to pursue a college degree, and you are now researching colleges and strategies. Perhaps you stumble on the method of testing out of classes using credit-by-exam tests. Arguments both for and against this learning style abound. While the flexible timeline for studying, the opportunity to save money, and the numerous study locations are all appealing, other opposing factors loom overhead like gargoyles.

Like most educational methods, there are challenges to overcome, especially in the beginning stages when everything is new and unfamiliar. These vague yet imposing concerns include the quality of education received, the acceptance of a degree earned off campus by future employers and schools, the impossibility of getting a degree "on your own," and the fear of missing the campus experience. These are valid concerns, and I will address each briefly now and again in more depth over the course of the book.

Accreditation

Something that was a significant hurdle for me to overcome and that is also a significant hurdle for students who are considering credit-by-exam testing is understanding accreditation: how colleges are regulated and legitimized. We hear of degree and diploma mills in the news, and many of us have received spam emails offering us a diploma *fast and for only $99.99!* This makes us wary of degrees that are earned 100% online or off campus. How can we know if these schools are legitimate? How will we know if our employer will accept our degree? And will our degree transfer to our post-grad school?

Answers to these questions are vital to off-campus learners because they enable students to construct their path to a degree such that their long-term goals are supported and furthered. These answers also give reassurance that going against the traditional college current is worthwhile, and they help immensely when explaining this "other path" to friends and acquaintances. Knowledge about college/university accreditation plays a dominant role in these answers, and it is so crucial that I've devoted chapter 9 to explaining and expanding on this topic.

No Profs?!

Another hurdle is studying without a professor's direct help. This is the defining difference between credit-by-exam tests and online courses, where the professor or other course leader is available for correspondence. When considering credit-by-exam tests without a teacher, students can feel they will have no one to turn to for help.

Today in our wonderfully connected and resourceful world, this worry is far from reality. Help is many times just a website away, whether it be the website of the college you plan to attend, a website of instructional videos, or a technical website designed to discuss difficult, detailed research. Off-campus students *build* their support framework, which can look surprisingly similar to the support framework of on-campus students. And for motivational and moral support from others using credit-by-exam tests, look no further than DegreeForum.net, an online discussion website devoted to both blended and completely off-campus learning.

The Campus Experience

A discussion of hurdles would not be complete without a discussion about missing the college experience by not being on campus. There are at least two ways to look at this. Each student will need to evaluate his college degree objectives to determine which strategy will benefit him most.

1) You decide that being on campus is the best way to reach your college goals. If your goals include living in a dorm, playing collegiate sports, performing research at a research institution, or studying with large numbers of students who attend the same school, these will be far easier to achieve on campus than off. However, being on campus doesn't preclude the use of credit-by-exam tests; you may want to use credit-by-exam testing to augment the credits you earn through on-campus classes. These exams can help you quickly complete introductory credit requirements and/or demonstrate language proficiency at your own pace and as your schedule allows.

2) You decide you want to blend traditions of college life with off-campus learning to create the ideal learning environment for you. This can vary from living off campus while taking online courses to solely using credit-by-exam testing to earn your degree. To do this, you find other ways to give yourself the on-campus opportunities you wish to experience while living and studying off campus. You could join a house with other students for a living atmosphere similar to a dorm, enroll in a non-collegiate athletic team for sports, or

start a college study group that is not school specific. You probably will have to work harder to create your own study atmosphere and agenda, but your reward is your schedule's personalization and flexibility. You also gain variety in the learning opportunities available as you glean resources from an assortment of colleges and organizations. With the exception of those individuals who don't live near enough to a college to attend in person, the learning options for off-campus students are just as broad as students living on campus.

When choosing one of the two strategies above, you will need to examine your college goals. It's important to include objectives that aren't directly related to the degree's cost or the courses studied. These more widespread goals may include regularly meeting new people, moving to a different town, being away from or staying close to parents, studying directly under a professor, joining a particular club, living in a new environment, and learning how to be a better self-learner. Outlining your college goals is key to helping you walk down the graduation aisle knowing that you have met your personalized objectives.

CREATING CUSTOMIZED COLLEGE GOALS

Outside-the-classroom learning can come through various activities including jobs, internships, family businesses, certifications earned from private companies, and self-directed study. Through off-campus learning, the student is tied far less to college schedules. He can learn at convenient times and places and study sporadically as his work, family, and health allows. For those of us who study more diligently with set deadlines or motivational goals, these are just a decision away.

Far from wandering through college quicksand, college off campus still gives deadlines, goals, and time frames. The only difference from traditional college is that *you* set these goals. Instead of using a schedule that was created by the college, you create a schedule to suit you. Two examples of your role in creating boundaries for your learning are choosing how many credit-by-exam tests to take per month (perhaps one every month) and deciding when you want to graduate (for example, in three years instead of four).

CREDIT-BY-EXAM TESTS

Before we go any further, please allow me to introduce you to two popular credit-by-exam tests. In essence, these tests are equivalent to testing out of a course: you study to acquire the knowledge you will need and then take the test to demonstrate that knowledge.

One of the most outstanding aspects of these tests is that it does not matter where you earned your knowledge. On the job, in a college class yesterday or twenty years ago, from life experience, or through self-directed study using a college textbook—regardless of how you learned it, your knowledge applies if it relates to the information covered by the test.

The following test brands are two of the most widely used credit-by-exam programs available. Taking a couple of exams offered by either brand will give you familiarity with credit-by-exam testing.

CLEP

What is CLEP? CLEP, the acronym for College Level Examination Program, is one of the many testing programs created by the College Board (some of their other programs include AP tests and the SAT). CLEP exams are accepted at over 2,900 colleges and universities around the world.

I consider CLEP tests to be gateway exams, because they are ideal for people new to testing out of classes and because the test-taking skills learned in a CLEP test apply to many other types of tests. CLEP exams can be used to test out of many of the lower-level courses that freshmen are required to take; students utilize CLEP titles such as Introductory Psychology, College Composition, College Algebra, and Information Systems.

CLEP tests last 90 minutes (except the 120-minute College Composition), and each test is worth 3-9 credits based on its difficulty, with most being worth lower-level credit (credit equating to a 100- or 200-level class). All CLEP tests are computer-based and scored between 20 and 80, with 50 being the typical score needed to earn credit. Each college sets the score required to earn credit for a particular test, but most follow the recommendations given by the American Council on Education (an organization that reviews college-level courses and provides recommendations as to how many credits each course should be worth).

CLEP exams are pass/fail, unless the college where you are sending your CLEP credits sets benchmarks that correspond to grades. This is rare, and most likely if you achieve a 50 or higher, you obtain credit. CLEP stores your scores for 20 years, which allows you to take tests prior to enrolling at any college and later request your scores to be sent to the college(s) of your choice when you are ready to enroll. Currently, CLEP exams cost around $110 apiece, with $80 dollars going directly to the College Board and the remaining $30 or so going to the test proctor.

DSST

DSST tests are identical in concept to CLEP tests but differ in scope and in their creator. DSST tests are produced by the Defense Activity for Non-Traditional Educational Support (DANTES) program, which is a branch of the Department of Defense. Although the tests were designed for military members, they are available to civilians as well and are administered at military bases, college campuses, and other testing locations.

The majority of DSST exams cover subjects different than those offered by CLEP. Of the 34 titles available, 9 titles are recommended by the American Council on Education to be worth upper-level credit, although the final say about the level of credit always depends on individual college policy. DSST tests are free for active military members, veterans, and some military family members, while civilians pay a fee similar to that of a CLEP test. DSST tests are given on the computer and are two hours in length.

Between CLEP and DSST, a significant portion of a student's degree can be completed via credit-by-exam. Most degrees require one or two years' worth of general education and free elective courses. These lower-level courses are ideal to test out of, allowing you to move on to higher-level subjects and courses that directly apply toward your degree's concentration. Blasting through lower-level requirements can promote the progress of nearly any student.

So where are these tests accepted? While CLEP is credited at over 2,900 institutions and DSST at over 1,900 institutions, there are three schools in particular that make it easy to transfer these tests into a degree.

THE BIG THREE: COSC, EC, & TESU

You guessed it—the Big Three are colleges. This needs some clarification as there is more than one set of "Big Three" colleges. You probably have heard of the Big Three referring to Harvard, Yale, and Princeton. However, when used in the context of distance learning, the Big Three refers to the Big Three colleges *of distance learning:* Charter Oak State College (COSC), Excelsior College (EC), and Thomas Edison State University (TESU). All three schools are devoted to online and off-campus students, and each school's policies are designed to benefit these students. One example of this is that all three schools have low residency requirements, meaning that few classes must be taken directly from the colleges and that the colleges accept a wide variety of transferred courses and tests, including CLEP and DSST tests. Each of the Big Three is regionally accredited, which is the highest level of accreditation granted in the United States (more about this in chapter 9).

While the above is just a short overview of the Big Three, you will find more information about each school in chapter 10, as these schools play a major role in helping students advance their education while taking advantage of a variety of learning methods.

CLIMBING THE EDUCATION LADDER

Higher education is almost always done sequentially. While a student can occasionally climb two rungs of the education ladder at the same time (such as when completing a combined bachelor's/master's program), more often, a student will need to climb every rung starting from the bottom.

When using off-campus learning, there is more flexibility to quickly complete the easier parts of the degree and linger on the areas of study that are most challenging, most pertinent to your end goal, or simply the most rewarding and enjoyable. This enables you to have more control regarding how long you remain on one rung before continuing to the next.

Even though education moves sequentially, sometimes life does not. You might decide to get a degree after years on the job, using the degree to demonstrate what you learned. Maybe you're like me when I graduated from high school: you aren't sure what field you will pursue, but you want to keep studying and achieve a degree without wasting money or time. Or perhaps you are moving more or less sequentially, and you need a degree to get the job you want. Distance learning can assist in all three situations and propel you toward deep, life-enriching education.

THE GOAL OF COLLEGE

The goal of college should not be just acquiring learning, but learning *how* to learn. I can stuff myself with facts and figures, ace my tests, and then walk out of a class and find I didn't really internalize what I thought I was learning. I could blame my memory, or I could seek out that lost information when I need it again.

This is why I love off-campus learning. More than saving money and time, it taught me the lifelong skill of *how to learn.* I know that I can tackle subjects I consider challenging, such as differential equations, thanks to the confidence I gained while studying calculus through reading, working problems, and finding answers to my questions.

If we know how to look for answers to our questions, we will never be stuck at one level of learning. Our memories may be poor, but if we know how to refresh and reclaim this information, we will not be without hope for expanding our knowledge. And, even more importantly, this relearning can be done in a way that is more memorable, engaging, and customized to our learning style, time schedule, and attitude.

Now that you have an introduction to credit-by-exam testing and some examples of how it can benefit differing student goals, we can explore specific off-campus alternatives that can be matched to both your available funds and time. I share my experience as an off-campus learner in the next chapter as one example of using credit-by-exam tests to reach college goals.

CHAPTER 2

THE FINISH LINE

Around the time I was roughly eight tests (worth a total of 24 credits) away from the 120 credits necessary to graduate, I could see the light at the end of the tunnel. This was the time to "hunker down," as my Grandma Vicky says, and plow through those last tests. Though I'm surrounded by college campuses, the nearest one to offer DSST tests is currently in Moses Lake, requiring a 120-mile car trip of just over two hours. Now, lest anyone think I had it rough, consider the students from around the globe who take an airplane to reach their testing center. That's a commute![6]

My last eight tests were all DSSTs, and I knew many trips to Moses Lake were in order. After the first of eight tests, I decided to try taking two tests in one trip. Though two tests in a day is not particularly outstanding, getting psychologically and logistically ready to take two tests in one day/trip is certainly challenging. First, I had to know the information for two subjects sufficiently and be prepared to test for both concurrently. This meant that I had to divide my study time judiciously and monitor when one subject was getting easier and more fun, which was my signal that I should divert my attention to the neglected subject.

After balancing my study budget, I was then ready to coordinate with the testing center. All DSST tests are proctored, and the testing candidate is monitored to insure test fairness and integrity. My typical DSST test day went like this:

6:00 a.m.   Rise, shine, eat, and collect flashcards and notes to study on the way.

7:00 a.m.   Hit the road. My mom or sister would usually drive, giving me time to study and limiting my road weariness.

9:30 a.m.   Begin Test #1. Rack brain for two hours and give strong focus, while reserving some energy for Test #2.

11:30 a.m. Quick snack in car, a short walk to ease stiffness, and a reboot for my mind.

12:00 p.m. And we're back...for Test #2. This one was harder because my brain was tired and my eyes more sensitive to the computer's glare, but easier because I already completed Test #1 (and passed!).

2:00 p.m.   Finally, done! At this point, I felt a mix of exhilaration for being the proud owner of six college credits and the exhaustion of a zombie-tester. Another two-hour drive and I would be home.

Here is a perfect time for me to note that what I did three times in my degree journey is not unique. There are hundreds of students out there tackling their degree in chunks and speeding their way to degree success, multiple tests at a time. DegreeForum.net is filled with results from students who charge into the testing center and emerge hours later with 3, 9, and even 36 credits to their name. It does get easier and I was not nearly as fatigued on the second round of tests as the first. However, I cannot minimize the effort that credit-by-exam testing requires. It is a commitment—a commitment to your goals and your future, a commitment to doing the best you can, and a commitment to the delayed gratification of some of your favorite activities while you instead study like mad (unless one of your favorite activities is studying like mad!).

Luckily, not all off-campus credit earning is as intense as described above. Those DSSTs were fulfilling the upper-level credits within the concentration of my social sciences degree. The tests *should* have been hard. However, not all of a degree is that difficult, off campus or on. Take free elective credits, for example. Here is where you get to explore areas outside your chosen field that may have no immediate value other than to complete your degree. These classes don't have to be "pull your hair out" intensity.

One thing is for sure: Preparing to graduate from college cannot be labeled as "relaxing" or "effortless." This final push to finish college takes coordination and concentration, whether on campus or off. In my case, I was working around Thomas Edison State University's graduation schedule (graduation is offered four times a year, with one cap and gown ceremony in New Jersey each September). To graduate, I first had to make sure that my degree plan was complete (which I worked out with an advisor). I then applied to graduate, mailed a check to the university, and waited...anxiously. Fortunately for me, Thomas Edison State was prompt about alerting me to my graduation status. Within two weeks of applying to graduate, I received an email acknowledging my graduation request. A second email a month later confirmed that I could and would indeed graduate on September 7, 2012.

I was thrilled that I had completed this four-year adventure and achieved my goal of earning a bachelor's degree. The best feeling came from knowing I had no debt because of my degree. *None.* I was able to pay cash using the savings I personally had set aside. I was able to do this largely because of my family. When I was around seven years old, my dad and mom began giving me an allowance in exchange for making my bed, setting the table, hand-washing dishes, etc. Forty percent of this weekly stipend went into a savings account. I also was given money at birthdays and Christmas to do with as I pleased. Since I lean towards being a penny pincher rather than a spendthrift, much of my gift money made it into my savings account. When I was 16, my savings were officially termed "College Savings." Even though it was my money, I do not feel that I put myself through college. It is only through the generosity of my family that I was able to pay for tuition, room, and board. My side of the bargain included not blowing my gift money and later choosing to commit to college.

So, what was my total college tab? My four-year, fully accredited social sciences degree cost me $9,552. This figure includes all my books and supplies, tuition, and graduation fees. Because I didn't need to live on or near a campus, and since I didn't want to move to New Jersey at the time, I chose to live with my parents. This in itself dramatically reduced the cost of my college encounter.

I estimate the cost paid by my parents for me to live at home for the 36 months (nine months for four years) of college between 2008 and 2012 at $11,500, making my average cost-per-year $2,875. This is substantial, but compare this to the average room and board paid by full-time college students at a four-year public school during the 2009-2010 school year: $8,162. Private school students paid $9,331. For the 2015-2016 school year, public school students paid $10,138, while private school students paid $11,516.[7] This is *per year*, and college isn't always completed in four years!

I am passionate about the financial benefits of off-campus college, even though saving money was not my singular reason to live at home or to earn a college degree off campus. The feeling you have when you graduate without debt is incredible. There is no aftertaste. There is no sorrow that comes after the euphoria of accomplishment. There is no interest and no paying twice for the degree you got only once.

And it's achievable. The possibility for this dream to become your own is there! There is a way to go to college and come out without debt, without strapping Dad and Mom, and without unnecessary heartache. This way isn't easy and it's definitely not fun and games. But it is rewarding and challenging. When students emerge from this college experience, diploma in hand, having taken a different path to reach the same goal, they begin their next phase in life with little or no debt, self-motivation skills, and habits beneficial to lifelong learning.

In the FAQ section for chapter 2 beginning on page 163 you can find the results of a few of the numerous studies that highlight the effects of student debt.

TAKEAWAY TIPS

- Though finishing a degree is not easy, completing this goal is worth the frustration and effort required.
- Living at home can save you money that can then be used to fund other adventures and goals, such as a master's degree, wedding expenses, a down payment on a house, a vacation, etc.

CHAPTER 3

FEES AND TACTICS

ere I will discuss five specific methods to save money while pursuing a college degree. There are numerous ways to tweak the traditional college learning format to facilitate more cost-effective learning. There are also many superb resources available to guide you during this endeavor.

Method 1: Postpone Enrollment

For the first three years of college, I was unenrolled. I spent my time studying and gaining credits without matriculating at a college. I was able to do this because most, if not all, credits earned through distance learning methods are kept on file for a set number of years. (CLEP, for example, keeps students' test scores on file for 20 years.) Postponing enrollment saved me over $7,500.[8] The disadvantages of being unenrolled were that I did not have access to detailed advisement or a personalized degree plan created by the college. However, I was, and continue to be, pleasantly surprised at the resources that are openly available to the unenrolled student. Here is an example:

Just before I enrolled, one of my biggest questions was if my CompTIA

A+ certification (a test measuring computer technician competency) would be accepted for credit at Thomas Edison State University. From information I found on the web, I could see this certification was equal to as many as nine credits depending on the college.[9] Naturally, I wanted to know how many credits I could expect to receive at TESU. While I was unenrolled, I sent TESU an email with this question. The university quickly responded to let me know that unfortunately, TESU did not accept the CompTIA A+ certification for credit. Though I was disappointed, knowing this information before enrolling allowed me to confidently move forward as I finalized my choice of school and look for other ways to earn credit for some of my computer knowledge (this turned out to be through CLEP).

While it may not be possible to precisely know until you enroll what credits will fulfill certain requirements in your degree, there is a cornucopia of information available that will give you a general, if not exact, plan to follow as you earn credit. A large selection of this information, especially regarding enrollment, can be found on DegreeForum.net. This is an internet forum run by InstantCert.com, an online business that offers credit-by-exam test preparation. The forum is open for anyone to view and post messages, with the exception of the Specific Exam Feedback section that is for InstantCert members only. Even excluding the Exam Specific section, DegreeForum.net is loaded with continually updated advice on what types of credit can be earned through which methods and where that credit can be applied. Here is where I found many of the answers I was looking for without having to contact TESU, such as how long the enrollment process generally takes; where CLEP, DSST, and other credit-by-exam tests are applied in a certain degree plan; and which degrees can be completed using credit-by-exam tests alone. These are just a few reasons I love DegreeForum.net, and I will continue to discuss the site's advantages in chapter 5.

My inquiry regarding CompTIA A+ introduced me to TESU's admissions counselors. As their name conveys, these college employees are there to instruct you through the application and enrollment process. But did you know they will also help with questions about the college's programs and policies before you enroll? Obviously, I don't recommend bombarding these people with inquiries, but students should be aware of this avenue for guidance. A counselor may be able to answer some of your more specific questions not answered on a college's website or elsewhere online.

Method 1 in a Nutshell:

FEES:	None.
COSTS:	Less guidance from the college.
SAVINGS:	Number of years working toward degree multiplied by enrollment cost for one year (for me, over $7,500).
SUMMARY:	Postponing enrollment is a genuine savings, since you only pay for enrollment when you truly need it.

Method 2: College Aid for Off-Campus Students

There are three types of student aid available: grants, scholarships, and loans. Grants and scholarships do not have to be repaid, meaning they are gift money. You will find varying criteria to be eligible for grants and scholarships. Loans are debt with interest, though sometimes the interest is deferred until the student graduates (as with some federal loans). Loans for education must be considered carefully, with regard to what your money is buying and what return your knowledge and potential earnings will bring. A common recommendation is to borrow no more than one year's wages to pay for a degree.

Students can receive financial aid even if they are off campus. The location of study is typically not the limiting factor when applying for grants, scholarships, and loans. Instead, factors influencing aid for off-campus students are enrollment status and the type of classes you plan to take. Most aid only becomes available once a student is enrolled, meaning that using Method #1 described above may decrease a scholarship or grant's applicability. However, considering that credits earned by students before enrollment usually have a low per-credit cost, this is not usually a problem. After completing these off-campus credits, students may finish their degree using online or on-campus classes from the school of their choice, at which point they can apply for financial aid.

Even when used to fund tuition and classes taken directly through a college, financial aid can prove to be less helpful than it appears, due to aid programs' specific specifications, such as a disbursement schedule or necessary course load.[10] Because there are so many variables with regard to aid, the challenge becomes finding aid that facilitates your goals.

Discover applicable aid through an internet search. Federal and state programs along with most institutions use the Free Application for Federal Student Aid (FAFSA) to determine your eligibility for aid. You can fill out this form online at www.fafsa.gov. Completing this form is an excellent way to learn which types of aid are available to you. If your household income prevents you from receiving aid, you can search for scholarships not tied to income that correspond with your hobbies, gender, age, or even height!

Thomas Edison State University, Excelsior College, and Charter Oak State College (the "Big Three") have in-house scholarships, and all three schools' aid programs begin with filling out the FAFSA. Each offers an array of scholarships with varying requirements and objectives.[11] Scholarship requirements change intermittently, and it's a good idea to check the appropriate college's website for the latest information.

Have you served in the military? You may want to search for financial aid solely available to military members, which includes their immediate family and veterans. Using an online search engine can disclose other websites devoted to military scholarship research and military scholarships themselves.

If you are an active duty, reserve, or National Guard military member, your CLEP, DSST, and some ECE (Excelsior College Exams) tests will be paid for by the government. Also eligible for the waived test fee are civilian employees and spouses of members of the Air Force Reserve, Army Reserve, and Coast Guard (active and reserve). Veterans can seek test fee reimbursement through the U.S. Department of Veterans Affairs (VA). While the government declines to pay for any test-taker's retake of the same test title, you can pay for the retry yourself. For more details about CLEP, see http://clep.collegeboard.org/military/. Regarding DSST, see http://getcollegecredit.com/test_takers/. Find veterans' reimbursement facts here: http://www.benefits.va.gov/gibill/national_testing.asp.

Because I had saved money for many years before I began college, I had cash set aside for my tests and enrollment fees, which meant I didn't explore my options for financial aid. Though I've always been aware of what a benefit this was, my post-degree research regarding financial aid has given me an even deeper appreciation for monetary reserves. Cash precludes loans and interest. Plus, by using credit-by-exam testing methods, your saved cash goes further. A $60-$100K degree achieved on campus is difficult to pay for with previously-saved cash (or any type of money for that matter), while a $10-$20K degree off campus is far more feasible to save for.

Jennifer Cook-DeRosa, author of *Homeschooling for College Credit*, looks at taking credit-by-exam tests as scholarships in and of themselves. She writes to a mother of an undergraduate son, "The average cost of a college degree at a public school without dorms/books is $30,000. At TESU, a rack rate BA degree is $40,200. Using ingenuity, resourcefulness, and hard work, your son's BA at TESU will be $4,147. By my math, that's a $36,000 scholarship!"[12]

For more information about scholarships, I recommend searching online, particularly DegreeForum.net.

Method 2 in a Nutshell:

FEES:	For grants and scholarships, none required to apply. For loans, interest payments and other charges.
COSTS:	Time and effort spent applying for financial aid, possible study constraints to receive aid, negatives associated with gifted/borrowed money, and loss of some freedom in study and work schedules.
SAVINGS:	Even without the necessary cash, it is possible to complete a degree.
SUMMARY:	Financial aid is a mixed bag: for some students it is a lifeline during their voyage, while other students may prefer to save or earn cash.

Method 3: Enrollment = Tax Write-Off

Your educational expenses may be tax write-offs once you enroll. Qualifying expenses include tuition but not books and supplies, just as it is for on-campus learners. To learn more about tax credits, you may want to research the Lifetime Learning Credit and the American Opportunity Credit.[13] Do remember to use these enrollment fees as tax deductions when you are enrolled.

Method 3 in a Nutshell:

FEES:	No fees other than enrollment itself.
COSTS:	None.
SAVINGS:	Varies.
SUMMARY:	Great if you can use it.

Method 4: CollegePlus

I wanted to achieve my degree cost-effectively and with a minimum of outside help. So, I planned my degree using only the degree plan on TESU's website and information from DegreeForum.net posts. It was a stretch for me to subscribe to the online study flashcards of InstantCert.com, and I would have spurned even this study resource in the name of saving money if my mom hadn't convinced me that it would be a helpful aid. Hindsight being 20/20, I see that my reluctance to get outside support *did* save me money, but this style of achieving a degree is certainly only one of many viable and economical options. Choosing and planning my degree using advice I found online was very cost-effective but time-consuming. If you are in the situation where your time is more valuable than money or you want a master blueprint to follow as you build your college degree, then College-Plus may be just the architect for you!

CollegePlus was co-founded in 2004 by Woody Robertson, Brad Voeller (distance learning advocate and author of the exceptional book for off-campus students, *Accelerated Distance Learning*), and Ryan Yamane. The company currently offers four programs. Unbound and Pathway are for students who want to quickly earn college credit, Prep is for high school students interested in earning dual credit, and Navigate is a three-month non-credit course connecting students with a mentor for creating a five-year life plan.

Both the Unbound and Pathway programs guide students as they earn their degree using credit-by-exam testing, online exams, and CollegePlus courses. Each student has access to a CollegePlus coach, who answers your questions, encourages you, and holds you accountable to your goals. Using CollegePlus gives you assistance in planning your degree, allowing you to customize what you learn within the degree's framework. Essentially, CollegePlus culls germane resources and methods targeted for learners who are willing to challenge the traditional college method, and then encourages and assists them throughout the process.

The Prep program is very similar to Pathway with the end goal being high school graduation and college preparation rather than a degree. Completion of Prep provides students with up to 18 college credits. The program also emphasizes self-motivation and a lifelong love for learning.

One of my favorite aspects about CollegePlus is the flexibility. CollegePlus understands that life doesn't stop while pursuing a degree. The years spent working on a degree are not exclusively filled by college. During those years, life goes on. There are family issues and celebrations, there are work opportunities, and there are other goals in progress. By utilizing your life experiences and expeditious learning methods, CollegePlus helps you earn a degree in complement to your other goals within the existing structure of your life. If you are excited about getting your degree off campus, online, or even on campus using some of the techniques I discuss in this book and decide to hire a mentor to guide you, visit https://collegeplus.org/.

Method 4 in a Nutshell:

FEES:	The two bachelor's degree programs, Unbound and Pathway, require a $1900 down payment with a $195 monthly subscription, plus course fees. Prep costs $350 with a monthly subscription fee of $145, plus book and course fees.[14]
COSTS:	Time and commitment are required to plan and coordinate your progress with a mentor.
SAVINGS:	You'll save time by having a personal coach to answer your questions and help create a degree plan. CollegePlus's familiarity with the policies of different schools (CollegePlus students have transferred their credits to over 100 colleges) may reduce your college expenses.
SUMMARY:	Analyze yourself. Do you work better having an experienced mentor? Is the money spent worth the guidance you'll receive? If yes, CollegePlus may be just the ticket.

Method 5: Study Smart

ed Distance Learning introduced my family to several key study materials. These programs can change your study habits forever! My mother purchased *Maximum Speed Reading* by Howard Berg and *Dynamic Memory and Study Skills* by Brad Voeller in my junior year of high school. All three of us—my 13-year-old sister, my mom and I—went through the courses together. To this day I use the memory tools and the speed reading skills advised in those two courses. I highly recommend them both for all off-campus learners.

A third resource that I can advocate with first-person experience is *Advanced Communication Series* taught by Andrew Pudewa. This program is suited for high school students, college students, and adults, and it provides a method for putting your thoughts on paper in a persuasive, informative way. I used these skills when taking the SAT and ACT tests in my junior year of high school and again during college. The program's tips and exercises apply easily to CLEP and DSST tests that require writing. Rather than let your voice be swallowed up in uncertainty or paralysis when faced with a five-paragraph essay, let your views be known through the power of your pen.

Method 5 in a Nutshell:

FEES:	*Maximum Speed Reading* costs around $90, *Dynamic Memory and Study Skills* retails for $99.95, and *Advanced Communication Series* is $69, but all three can be found used online at significantly lower prices (look for used sets that include both the course CDs and the companion workbook, which may also be on CD).
COSTS:	It takes time and effort to learn the techniques presented.
SAVINGS:	The efficient life skills learned through the three programs will save you time and money throughout life.
SUMMARY:	What you gain from these three courses may be the most functional and valuable information of your entire degree.

The Little Things

I present these tips near the beginning of the book to show some of the methods used in distance learning. These methods are the seemingly little things that can make the degree process much more enjoyable and bring degree completion to reality. While using these methods does require varying amounts of effort, the reward and best part of these techniques is the lifelong benefits they provide. Far from being a skill set that loses its applicability after college, these techniques carry over into everyday life. If I use an analogy of building a house to represent completing a degree off campus, these tips are the foundation that makes the entire house possible. In the next two chapters, I discuss the cornerstones that stand on this foundation.

TAKEAWAY TIPS

- Wait to enroll until you're ready to take a course from a college or you're ready to graduate.
- Debt is not the only way to pay for education. You may want to save cash or look for scholarships instead.
- Once you are enrolled, remember to look into using your college expenses as tax write-offs.
- If you decide that planning your college road map yourself is not something you want to tackle, consider hiring a mentor from CollegePlus.
- Take time to equip yourself with learning tools you can use throughout life.

CHAPTER 4

INTRODUCING CLEP TESTS

College Level Examination Program (CLEP) tests are standardized exams developed by the College Board, the organization who also publishes AP tests and the SAT. For over 40 years, CLEP tests have been offered to students who wish to show they have acquired knowledge that is equivalent to the information learned in a college classroom. This knowledge may have come from independent study, advanced high school courses, work experience, or college classes with non-transferable credits. CLEP tests give students of all ages a way to demonstrate that their learning is at college level and worthy of credit. CLEP banks your test scores (meaning they are on file and ready to be sent to the college of your choice) for 20 years.[15]

CLEP tests are one of the two most common types of credit-by-exam tests. (The other type will be discussed in the next chapter.) Because of the widespread usage of CLEP tests in off-campus degrees and because the tests are accepted at over 2,900 colleges and universities, these tests are an excellent way to explore credit-by-exam testing and decide if this credit-earning method suits your learning style. CLEP tests form the basis of credits for the majority of off-campus degree plans. Taking these tests can aid in preparing for other college tests by introducing typical testing procedure, rewarding consistent study skills, and providing knowledge to build upon in higher-level studies. Thus, this chapter will present some basics about this type of testing and outline the study strategies that enabled me to take (and earn credit for) 17 CLEP titles.

So, how did I utilize CLEP exams? CLEP exams enabled me to test out of all my entry-level general college courses using the following CLEP titles: English Literature, Humanities, Social Sciences and History, Natural Sciences, College Mathematics, and English Composition with Essay (which has been replaced by College Composition). Each title is worth three or six credits. Because most of the test content is covered in high school, these six tests are a perfect choice for 8-12th graders and adult students.

I took Natural Sciences and College Mathematics in my senior year of high school. Preparing for those two tests wasn't much additional work since I was already studying the subjects in school, and I was thrilled to begin earning credits for college. My sister, Lauren Anne, eclipsed me by completing five exams during high school for a total of 24 credits. Say a student took all six general exams in high school and earned 30 credits; since a bachelor's degree is typically 120 credits, the student would have completed one year of college!

If it is so feasible to test out of the first year of college, why isn't it more popular? When I think back to my reservations about taking CLEP tests, I remember several reasons. Like most high school seniors, I was eager to first finish high school and then move on to college. The time and effort needed to find a test center, research the tests, and then actually sit for the tests seemed to be more hassle than the credit was worth. Frankly, it sounded like drudgery. Furthermore, I had not decided which college I would be attending nor what degree I would pursue, so I felt unsure of which CLEP exams to take.

Other reasons that hold students back from CLEP tests are that they would rather go on campus to take courses, their advisors and mentors aren't promoting CLEP tests, or the whole thing sounds just too good to be true. To complicate matters further, these concerns are only a fraction of those faced by students during the transition from high school to college. The profusion of options available and the numerous decisions to be made can make it difficult to identify the best route, let alone one customized to the student's particular situation.

For me, another deterrent to completing credit-by-exam tests in high school was that I held a stigma toward students who took college classes

ge 17 or 18. In my teenage mind, I thought that college was some-
be tackled as a young adult once secondary education was com-
ow I realize that social and maturity issues aside, college-level
knowledge is appropriate for those who are searching for it, regardless of
their age.

After one or two CLEP tests, I had changed my tune about earning credit in high school, as I found that many of my reservations about CLEP exams
just weren't valid. Locating a test center is only a website away. Learning the
test material? CLEP test resources are plenteous, some for a reasonable fee
and some for free. For the general tests, the information needed for each
test is very similar to the information learned in corresponding high school
classes. This information is basic, common, and standardized, leaving me
almost entirely ready to test without extra study beyond my high school
courses.

For students who want to begin earning general credits without a specific degree plan, credit-by-exam tests are perfect! By using CLEP exams
to test out of a college class, you avoid paying college tuition until you are
ready to take online or on-campus classes and/or graduate. Adult learners
can prepare by honing in on the areas of the exam that are most difficult for
them, skimming through what they already know, and skipping the potentially inconvenient classroom schedule.

In general, CLEP tests will suit you best if:
- You are willing to structure your own studying
- You want to save money or time
- You are able to take charge of your education

If there is even a slim possibility that you could use the credits offered by
CLEP testing, I encourage you to take at least one CLEP test. After one or
two tests, you will know if this method of credit earning will help you meet
your college goals. Here's how to get started:

CLEP TESTING STEP-BY-STEP:

1. What Is Your College's CLEP Policy?

Visit the website of the college or colleges where you plan to earn your degree. Find their policies for accepting credit-by-exam tests. I've found that using the search bar available on most college websites with keywords "CLEP" or "transfer credit" will help you locate the school's CLEP policies.

Verifying these policies before taking a CLEP exam is one of the most crucial ways to save yourself time, money, and frustration. Common CLEP protocol set by colleges includes a minimum credit-earning score and a cap on how many CLEP credits can be transferred. Some schools have very open protocol, granting credit for any of the CLEP exams that will apply to your degree plan. Other colleges are more selective in the number or type of CLEP exams that can be transferred. Knowing your college's exact requirements can alleviate unpleasant surprises later.

2. Find Your Test Center

Use the College Board's website to find your closest test center: http://clep. collegeboard.org/search/test-centers. Don't despair if there isn't a testing site in your town. Thanks to the reasonable rate of CLEP tests, you may be able to add in travel costs and still save over a traditional course. Call the potential test center to verify that their information on CLEP's website is current, and ask how far in advance you will need to schedule an exam. You can also get directions to the test center and find out the test center's proctor fee and accepted forms of payment.

3. How to Choose a Test

Decide which test you'll tackle first. You can view the available CLEP exams here: http://clep.collegeboard.org/exam. Currently, CLEP offers 33 exams stretching over five subject areas. For your first test, pick a subject that interests you and that will benefit your degree plan. If you don't have a degree plan, you may want to choose one of the six general exams. Studying for the general exams may prepare you for other tests with related material. If you choose to take a CLEP covering a favorite subject rather than a general exam, the credits you earn may apply toward your free elective requirements. I recommend beginning with an easier CLEP test as your initiation into the CLEP testing procedure, but if the only test you need to take is a doozy, study hard and take it anyway. The only way to fail this step is not to choose a test at all.

Because choosing which test to take first can be a major snag for a student new to CLEP, let's simplify this process with some hypothetical examples:

- Scenario one: Say you would like to enter the field of nursing and become a registered nurse. As you complete your RN certification prerequisites, you may decide to concurrently earn an associate or bachelor's degree. Nursing degree plans usually include some general education credits. If the school offering the degree program accepts CLEP tests, you would be able to use CLEP tests for these general education courses and, if applicable, free elective credits.

- Scenario two: You are an American history buff. You are considering a college degree in the future, but you're not sure exactly when you will enroll. If you are interested in showing that what you have learned is applicable to a degree, you might take CLEP's History of the United States I, and History of the United States II, each worth three credits. Thanks to your cache of American history knowledge, these tests shouldn't be rigorous. (Having taken both of these tests myself, I can vouch for the test material covering straightforward and general information.) Your history hobby has just enabled you to earn six credits that are accepted at over 2,900 colleges!

- Scenario three: You are a college-bound high school student. You may not have decided on a major, but the college you are planning to attend accepts CLEP exams. My recommendation would be to take the corresponding test for subjects you are currently studying, as well as tests covering subject areas in which you excel. What are the possible outcomes of taking CLEP tests in high school? If in the end you decide to attend a college that doesn't accept CLEP, you may not be able to gain credit. However, the knowledge and skills you learn while studying for your CLEP tests may improve your score on college entrance and placement exams, not to mention the improvement of your general life knowledge. If you do attend a college that accepts CLEP tests, you will likely be able to use your credits toward the general education and free elective areas of your degree, which are typically lower level. A surprising number of degrees have similar credit requirements at this level. In some cases, your CLEP scores may allow you to earn credits equivalent to over two years of college!

Where Will My First CLEP Test Fit into My Degree Plan?

To fit your CLEP test to your degree plan, first find the test's college course equivalent. There are two ways to go about this, and the method you choose will depend on your enrollment status. If you are enrolled and you can't find where a specific CLEP test would apply or what college course is its equivalent, then you can ask the college directly. Typically, these questions are directed to your advisor, whom you can contact through the college's ticket system, email, etc.

If you are not enrolled, determining which CLEP test is equivalent to which college course and where the test fits into your degree plan is challenging. Two places to begin the search are DegreeForum.net and the Degree Forum Wiki (which are discussed in more detail later).[16] On DegreeForum.net you can search for the name of the CLEP test you are trying to implement into your degree, or you can search for the college course you wish to test out of using CLEP. You may also want to search for DegreeForum.net users pursuing the same degree plan as you. Degree Forum Wiki offers user-submitted degree plans that show exactly what tests were used to complete a specific degree.

This step is one of trial and error, where you must tentatively put together a list of exams you think will satisfy the degree requirements, and then research to see if those exams will actually fit. With your list in hand as a starting point, you can then use the new information you find as your journey progresses to tweak this list as necessary. As soon as you enroll, you can discuss the list with an advisor, who can tell you exactly where your tests will apply to your degree and what exams you will need to complete your degree.

While this may sound touch-and-go, there are actually enough sample degree plans and user-supplied information to put together a plan with a high degree of accuracy. Plus, if you have a question about how to fulfill a specific degree requirement, you may be able to ask your perspective college before you enroll, even though the college is under no obligation to help you plan your degree since you are not paying for that service. At the same time, the college understands that you need to know *how* you will be able to fulfill degree requirements when determining which college you will attend. Thus, while the college will not put together a degree plan for you until you enroll, the school may be willing to answer a few limited questions regarding specific requirements.

4. Study Resources

Congratulations! You've just passed the first hurdle of CLEP testing: the beginning. Now that you have your heading, let's move on to studying for the exam. There are thousands of resources online and in print, from free study guides to expensive tutorials. Here is an opportunity to strike a balance between the expense, quality, and quantity of resources. Harmonizing these three aspects includes: studying appropriately using enough sources to cover the test without overwhelming yourself with materials; and using practice tests to gauge your readiness for the test and to measure the applicability of the information you are learning to the test itself. Begin by viewing the exam details for your test, which are available on CLEP's website. Think of these details as a bare-bones study guide, where you are told what topics comprise the test, and you get to decide how to internalize that information.

I now list some targeted ways to learn the information you will need to know when taking a CLEP test. I enjoyed using a variety of materials, including textbooks, study guides, online material, and computerized curriculum. This diversity assisted in providing a well-rounded education and helped me to stay excited about learning.

Alleydog.com (http://www.alleydog.com/): a website filled with material for psychology students. Here you can find information about psychology degrees, and what's more pertinent, information about psychology itself in class notes style. While I agree with the website's advice that these notes do not replace taking your own notes, having an additional set of notes to peruse and review can be useful for committing information to memory.

CliffsNotes (http://www.cliffsnotes.com/): study guides and online website. These study guides are another way to learn and review information pertinent to CLEP. While I didn't use CliffsNotes during college, my sister found them helpful during her studies. You may enjoy using these study guides to supplement your current materials as a change of pace.

Comex (http://www.comexsystems.com/): a brand of study guides whose topical books include both review information and a practice test. I have not used these guides, and some of them were published several years ago, so you will want to check for reviews (on DegreeForum.net, Amazon, etc.) to judge their relevancy.

DegreeForum.net (www.degreeforum.net): an internet forum owned by InstantCert Academy. The forum is completely free and open to the public, with the exception of the Specific Exam Feedback area of the forum, which is only available to InstantCert subscribers. DegreeForum.net is the single most beneficial site to the off-campus student. Here you can chat with other distance learners, read about common problems, and be advised of changes to tests and college policies. DegreeForum.net helped me choose the order to take my tests, create my degree plan, learn of new types of tests, and stay motivated.

One advantage of the site's internet forum structure is its relevance to many types of people. Even if you aren't keen on posting regularly, you can still benefit from DegreeForum.net. In my case, I typically used the forum as a lurker, as shown by my post count of two as an undergrad. My modus operandi was to use the search function to find another user's post regarding the same problem I had (and I rarely failed to locate someone who had already asked my question) and then learn from the responses. If you try this technique, keep an eye on the date of the posts. DegreeForum.net has been around long enough that you can run into outdated information.

On the other hand, if you are looking for an interactive and supportive community, you can find that here, too. Cultivated by dedicated DegreeForum.net users who post daily, an active volley of ideas, opinions, and research is available. The ever-increasing number of posts regarding credit-by-exam testing has improved the likelihood of finding another student who is working toward or has already finished the same degree from the same school as you. Just in my years of using DegreeForum.net, I've seen more and more students posting the list of exams they took to earn their degree. These degree plans can form the basis of your own degree plan, saving you time and allowing you to build on others' research.

As an example of the advice available on DegreeForum.net, you can view this post by a student who earned over 90 credits in about seven months! http://www.degreeforum.net/excelsior-thomas-edison-charter-oak-specific/17980-my-degree-plan-tesc-progress.html Here she lists the specific study resources she used to complete more than 20 exams. Her notes can be a starting point for your own study and save you from beginning your search for relevant resources at square one.

DegreeForum.net's Specific Exam Feedback: an area of DegreeForum.net that is only viewable by current InstantCert members. The Specific Exam Feedback section has an individual thread for nearly every CLEP test, as well as other types of credit-by-exam tests. In each thread, you'll usually find references for study materials and practice tests, as well as the results from testers who've completed the exam. The accuracy of the posts in this section almost justifies the cost of joining InstantCert.

Finding the Specific Exam Feedback section was tricky for me as a newbie. To locate this section, first make sure you are subscribed to InstantCert. Then, log in to DegreeForum.net. You may be redirected to the forum home page, but if not, simply click on the DegreeForum.net logo on the left or type "www.degreeforum.net" in your browser's address bar. From there you will see the link to the Specific Exam Feedback threads.

Finish College Fast (http://finishcollegefast.com/): a website offering study guides for all 33 CLEP titles. I have not used this company's products, but there are reviews available on DegreeForum.net. At $35.97, the cost makes this course a little more of an investment, which may be worthwhile if you are trying to achieve more comprehensive study. Because there are so many CLEP resources available, before choosing this course you may want to weigh it against other resources.

Free-Clep-Prep (http://www.free-clep-prep.com/): a website with resources for students taking CLEP, DSST, and Excelsior Exams. The force behind the website is Justin Orgeron, an avid test-taker and distance learning advocate with a military background. He has devoted the site to helping fellow test-takers. Justin ranks the difficulty of each exam compared to the other CLEP/DSST/Excelsior exams, compiles links to resources, and offers general information about the off-campus style of earning college credit. One thing I love about Free-Clep-Prep is the free practice tests available for a select number of CLEP and DSST exams. These tests are full length and designed to be very similar to the actual exam.

For additional study, Free-Clep-Prep offers Quick Prep Packages for $15.99 that contain a Quick Prep Study Guide, a professionally-narrated MP3 version of the guide, and two practice tests beyond the free one. For some test titles, only a study guide is available; this costs $8.99. When you are preparing a roadmap of how you will complete your CLEP test, be sure to check in with Free-Clep-Prep to take advantage of the excellent resources compiled on the website.

InstantCert Academy (http://www.instantcert.com/): a company offering study information covering 25 of the current 33 CLEP tests.[17] InstantCert uses an online flashcard format as their primary teaching method. For $20 per month or $108 for 6 months, you have access to their complete collection of flashcards—a convenient feature, especially if you are studying more than one test at once. InstantCert has been developing test preparation content since 2002, and their resources are extremely helpful because they are meticulously tailored to specific exams. Subscribing to InstantCert also allows you to view the Specific Exam Feedback section of DegreeForum.net (see above).

Khan Academy (https://www.khanacademy.org/): a nonprofit website filled with free video tutorials on subjects ranging from music to computing to math. The Academy was started in 2006 by Salman Khan, a former hedge-fund manager who quit his job to pursue what became the Academy's mission statement: "A free, world-class education for anyone, anywhere." Navigating the user-friendly website is quite intuitive, and within a subject, videos are ordered to reflect increasing difficulty, meaning you can start learning wherever is conducive for you.

While there are videos created expressly for some exams, such as the SAT and the GMAT, currently there are no videos specifically for CLEP tests, so you will need to browse for content relevant to your test title. Use the Knowledge and Skills Required (the list of subject material covered on a specific CLEP exam, available on CLEP's website) to compare the topics you need to know with the available videos.

Local Library: Libraries can be a way to borrow a textbook for use during your study rather than buying it outright. Throughout my degree journey, I was continually surprised by how many fabulous and useful resources were available at the public libraries in my area. This is due in part to my access to both the city and county library districts. The county library district includes Walla Walla Community College's library, which greatly augmented the types of books available at the city's public library. If you have admission to a college library, this can be a great place to find education-related materials. Do you have more than one library in your locale? You may benefit from being able to search multiple library catalogs at once using http://www.worldcat.org/.

My strategy for using the library was to first gather resource ideas from CLEP's study resources listed online for each exam and from DegreeForum. net, and then search for those resources using the libraries' online catalogs. I was able to obtain quite a few of my materials this way. Also while searching the catalog, I would type in the exam's subject and view the general results. Sometimes a *Dummies* book or other layman's book popped up, and I would use it for supplemental study. These simpler or slower-paced books can be lifesaving if your primary textbook becomes esoteric or progresses too quickly.

McGraw-Hill Online Learning Center: online collections of notes, glossaries, and other resources compiled around McGraw-Hill textbooks. Each collection contains supplementary material designed to complement a specific textbook. Each textbook has its own website. Even though this website doesn't provide the complete textbook for free, you may find a glossary or quiz beneficial. Finding these textbooks without their direct links can be difficult. One solution is to use a search engine with the keywords "McGraw Hill" and the subject of your test.[18]

My Education Path (http://myeducationpath.com/prepare_exams/4/ CLEP.htm): a website that can be of assistance when searching for study materials. Here you will find a well-organized list of resources for almost all of the CLEP exams. Each CLEP exam is matched to free online college courses offered by educational websites like Saylor Academy, edX, Alison, and others. If you enjoy having a course outline to follow while you prepare for a CLEP test, this website may be useful.

Official CLEP Website (http://clep.collegeboard.org/): the official homepage of CLEP. For essential CLEP information, including test descriptions, official practice tests, test centers, and a list of colleges that accept CLEP, this is the place to start.

Peterson's DOD MWR Library (http://www.nelnetsolutions.com/dod/): a compendium of resources offered to the military and their families. I have read good things about this collection, especially the included access to Peterson's pretests. Regardless of activation status (active, retiree, contractor, or civilian), all service members (Army, Marine Corps, Navy, Air Force, Coast Guard, National Guard, and Reserve) and their families are eligible. Free registration is required.

Podcasts: a (usually audio) program that can be downloaded and played on your computer, MP3 player, etc. Education-related podcasts can be found for nearly all platforms and media devices. Using podcasts, you can learn while exercising, driving, or getting ready in the morning! To increase learning retention, take notes while you listen.

REA Study Guides (http://www.rea.com/clep): This brand of study guides was one of my favorite CLEP resources. Unlike other study resources that strictly offer practice questions without teaching the information needed for the test, REA study guides include the information you will need to know along with practice tests. These guides differ from a college textbook in that the information is condensed and explicitly curated to teach the topics that are specified in the CLEP test syllabus. Because of this, you may need to supplement REA guides with information ranging from a simple online definition of an unknown acronym to a systematic study of the entire subject in uncondensed form using a textbook.

REA publishes *CLEP Core Exams*, which includes study material and practice tests for the following CLEP exams: College Composition & College Composition Modular, College Mathematics, Social Sciences & History, Humanities, and Natural Sciences. For the other CLEP exams, including the language tests, each title has its own REA preparation guide. Most of the exam titles have a pair of resources:

- a printed book of review information with one or more full-length practice tests
- an online component called the REA Study Center (or Online Test Package for some tests), which includes a diagnostic test that helps you pinpoint the areas you need to learn and two full-length practice tests modeled to simulate the real test (the online Study Center

can be purchased separately, if desired, or it may be included for free with the printed book)

My favorite aspect of REA's guides is the detailed explanation of every answer; if you answer a problem incorrectly, REA shows you how to arrive at the correct answer and why the other choices are wrong. REA's practice tests are carefully designed to be as close to the real thing as possible, and their computer-based practice tests feel like the actual exam. REA Study Guides are so handy that I wish they were offered for other credit-by-exam tests besides CLEP.

SparkNotes (http://www.sparknotes.com/): printed study guides and a study website. Though none of the content is specifically designed for CLEP tests, the website offers study material and practice questions relating to topics covered by CLEP. I used the practice questions during some of my history studies, and I enjoyed having a way to gauge how many facts and themes I was retaining. I mention this resource with a caveat: The website has a SparkLife section covering popular books, movies, and relationships that is advertised around the website via a sidebar, which can be distracting. However, the practice questions were so effective that I learned to ignore the enticing headlines and articles.

Testing & Education Reference Center: an online collection of college and career materials including e-books, résumé builders, and practice tests for CLEP, DSST, and other tests. The test preparation materials are by Peterson's, so this collection includes free access to their CLEP practice tests. Typically this group of resources is made available to libraries through a state-wide program. You should be able to find out if your state offers this Reference Center through an online search using the terms "Testing & Education Reference Center" and the name of your state. Some colleges offer these study resources to their students, so once you enroll, you may have access through your college. Also, DegreeForum.net users keep an eye out for new ways anyone can access the Reference Center; you can search for their posts on DegreeForum.net. (If you aren't able to access the Reference Center, the practice tests are available for purchase directly from Peterson's.)

Textbooks: For a few of the CLEP subjects, such as precalculus and calculus,

I opted to use a textbook to learn the information needed for the test. This was mostly when I was learning a subject for the first time. Using a textbook allowed me to build my understanding of the topic gradually, rather than diving into a test prep book, which is often formatted under the assumption that the student already knows the subject and is strictly studying as a review. I highly recommend using a textbook for the subjects that you know very little about or when you aren't able to readily find a suitable test prep book.

Which textbook should you choose? CLEP's study resources for each exam (available online) suggests a list of textbooks that can be used, which is a nice starting point in the textbook search. For textbooks not on this list, it can be helpful to compare the test's content breakdown with the table of contents in the textbook to verify that the textbook covers what you need to know.

There is rarely a need to buy a full-priced text, thanks to websites like Half.com, eBay, Amazon, and the myriad of other websites selling used textbooks. It is necessary to check the date of publication—older textbooks are fine, but you will want to get a book that covers current test content. Equally as important is finding a text that you can enjoy. If you like pictures, graphs, and relevant sidebars, look for a text with these features. Conversely, if you prefer to focus on the facts and internalize what you are learning through practice problems and solutions, look for this style of text. Because CLEP tests focus on information that is commonly taught in college classrooms around America, the majority of textbooks available for your subject will cover the information you need to know.

Wikipedia (http://www.wikipedia.org/): a free, user-created online encyclopedia. As a supplemental study resource, I found Wikipedia quite effective, though the information available is usually far more detailed than what is required in the test. Sister site Wikibooks.org can also be used to find study books.

My favorite resources are the CLEP Official Study Guide, InstantCert, DegreeForum.net, Free-Clep-Prep, and REA guides.

Because achieving success in credit-by-exam tests rests heavily on efficacious study, chapter 7 is curated to include study methods as well as motivational tips that I found helpful.

5. *Sources for Pretests*

It's time to put a powerful tool into play: practice tests. Practice tests are the best way to become familiar with the tests beforehand. The biggest benefit from practice tests is getting an idea of what type of information will be on the actual test. Practice tests also let you rehearse the CLEP test-taking strategy of answering every test question. When the actual CLEP tests are scored, points are not deducted for wrong or skipped answers, meaning it is to your advantage to answer all the questions even if you have to guess.

Practice tests are available from a variety of sources. Start with the sample questions directly from CLEP's website, as there are around seven free practice problems per exam. My sister and I both found these online sample questions and the *CLEP Official Study Guide* practice test questions to be extremely similar to the actual test questions, which is logical since both come directly from the College Board.

When exactly should you take a pretest? Some recommend taking the pretest first, before any study, to show you what the test will be about. Though I prefer to do general study first and then test what I've learned, I have noticed that as soon as I take a practice test, my learning is calibrated to the actual material and I more readily pick out the information I will need to know. So, don't wait; take a practice test!

My Favorite CLEP Pretest Resources:

CLEP Official Study Guide (book): a collection of practice tests, one for each of the 33 CLEP exams. Each practice test contains 50-105 questions. At $24.99, this book is a terrific deal if you plan to take three or more CLEP tests (you can download the practice test for an individual test subject for $10.00 each). The *CLEP Official Study Guide* can be purchased from http://clep.collegeboard.org and through booksellers. While the study guide does not teach the content covered in the tests, it gives an accurate view of *what* content will be on the test. It also has general CLEP test-taking advice.

CLEP Website Resources (http://clep.collegeboard.org/exam): Here you can find a few practice questions not included in the *CLEP Official Study Guide*, a list of textbooks used by colleges to teach the material covered in the exam, and online study resources.

Individual Official Practice Tests (http://clep.collegeboard.org/exam): official practice tests sold separately online in digital book format for $10.00 each. These are a good deal if you only take one or two CLEP tests.

Finish College Fast (http://finishcollegefast.com/): I recommend this site for the few free sample questions provided. To find them, click on study guide for the topic you are interested in and then click "Free Sample CLEP Questions Online." (Not all topics have free sample questions.)

Free-Clep-Prep (http://www.free-clep-prep.com/): As mentioned under CLEP Resources above, this website offers CLEP practice tests, currently for 12 titles.

Peterson's Exams (http://www.petersons.com/college-search/clep-practice-test.aspx): practice tests for every CLEP exam except the German language exam and College Composition Modular (the practice test for College Composition might be useful for this one). For each subject, you can buy a 90-day access pass to three full-length practice exams for $19.95. Since I didn't learn about these practice tests until after I finished my degree, I haven't used them, but they were extremely instrumental for my sister. She reports that they are quite comparable to the real tests. One of her favorite features is the opportunity to go over questions answered incorrectly. If you've only used paper practice tests, a Peterson's exam is a great way to gain computer-based test-taking experience. Check out the reviews of these practice tests on DegreeForum.net by searching for "Peterson's." The Testing & Education Reference Center and Peterson's DOD MWR Libraries Education website (both mentioned under CLEP resources) include free access to Peterson's CLEP practice tests.

6. Return to Your Study

Evaluate your weak areas made evident by the pretest. Try some different learning strategies if you aren't retaining the material (flashcards, mnemonics, essays, verbalization, etc.).

7. Take Another Pretest

If available, use a different pretest than the one used in Step 4. An internet search for "CLEP practice tests" can unearth other tests and reviews.

8. Are You Ready to Take the Test?

Time to make a judgment call: Are you close? Is your pretest score high enough that you feel comfortable going into the test center? Weigh your options here. Is your goal to know everything possible about this subject, or is this a periphery course required to complete your degree? If you are anxious to test as soon as possible but your pretest scores are below 60-80% correct, I recommend either a study blitz where you block out distractions and study as quickly and ferociously as you can or a study plan including a target testing date and a daily study time quota.

However, if you are like me and tend to procrastinate on scheduling the test even after careful study, remember two things: 1) CLEP tests are pass/fail: you do not receive a grade, and there is no bonus from CLEP or the college for a high or perfect score; 2) If you fail the first time, you can retake the same exam in three months.

When studying for a CLEP test, it can be hard to decide how deep to investigate the subject. Take human growth and development, for example. A person could devote her whole life to learning about this subject and still have more to learn. It's also a fascinating topic that broadly relates to our everyday life and the lives of those we love. In preparing for this subject's CLEP test, I found a seemingly infinite amount of study resources: books, tapes, online articles, academic journals, quizzes, and charts. Where would my studying end?

To answer this question, I chose between two goals: deep, comprehensive research or a focused inquiry for the knowledge needed to satisfy the test and propel me three credits closer to my degree. This same decision between goals buffeted me on nearly every one of the tests I took, and it is a quandary not unique to the world of credit-by-exam tests. This is something we face in daily learning, whether it be speaking a new language, preparing to be a parent, or studying our world. We know that there are enormous benefits from lifelong and continual learning, but inordinate focus on acquiring more learning without an objective can derail us from achieving our goals. Studying for credit-by-exam tests motivated me to learn how to study toward a singular goal (the test) and to keep my studying precise and coordinated. I use this skill frequently.

For subjects you find fascinating, why not continue studying them after taking the test or after you finish your degree?

9. Call Your Test Center

For your first test, it's wise to call between two to four weeks before your preferred test date. Make a note of the center's typical waiting period. The test center here in Walla Walla usually needed less than one week's prior notice, but other test centers may need a minimum of two weeks. If you're in doubt, call in advance!

10. Review

Review any weak areas, but don't over study. For me, I relaxed my study the day before the test and tried to avoid staying up late to cram. (I did do that for one test. Even though I achieved a credit-earning score roughly equal to my other tests, one experience with this study style was enough for me.)

11. Testing Day!

Follow typical testing procedure by arriving slightly early, wearing layers, adhering to test rules, and most of all, giving the test your all! Remember that it is in your best interest to answer every question, regardless if it's a guess. Scores are given when the test is completed, except for tests containing a writing component, which is scored by a qualified reviewer. If you choose, CLEP will send your test score automatically to the college of your choice for free at the time of testing. At the beginning of the test, you will have the opportunity to select which college you want to receive your score. If you do not want your score sent to any college on the day of the test, simply select "Do not send." CLEP will bank your score, and you can later request that all your scores be sent to the college(s) of your choice. The fee to send your collective scores to one college is $20.

CLEP tests are 90 minutes each, except the College Composition test

(120 minutes) and the College Composition Modular test (90 minutes with the optional addition of two essays in 70 minutes). Even if you absolutely hate tests, the most you will have to endure is three hours to collect credit. Plus, if you complete the exam before the time is up, you can usually leave as soon as you are finished. Remember that the test is just a short snippet in time, but it will take you a long step toward your goal.

12. Celebrate and Review

No matter what your score is, commend yourself for trying something new and challenging! Review your study habits and make note of what was easy to recall during the test. How did you internalize that knowledge? What information was most difficult to recall? Could improved study habits have helped your confidence or your score? I found it helpful to write a short review of the test, including what resources I had used and what I could have done differently, even if I passed the test. This knowledge helped me when I went to study similar topics, and it helped my sister when she took the same test and wanted to know what I had used to study. I was surprised at how fast I would forget what the test was like and how I had prepared. As for your test scores, CLEP holds them on file for 20 years, so whether you are on a 1½-year degree schedule or an eat-the-elephant-one-bite-at-a-time degree schedule, your hard-earned credits will be there when you need to transfer them. To do this, simply fill out the form available on the College Board website.[19]

Listed on page 185 you will find "My CLEP Test Reviews," where I share the individual resources I used for ten of the CLEP tests titles I took.

THE COST OF CLEP TESTS

To put the cost of CLEP testing in perspective, let's compare the expense of a one-semester general education course, say Introductory Psychology, taken three different ways. For the sake of simplicity, I will disregard living expenses and books.

I begin with the cost of attending a public college as an in-state student, using Washington State University as my example. According to their website, I can expect to pay $10,984 for my in-state tuition and mandatory fees for 20-36 credits in the 2016-2017 academic year (i.e., two semesters).[20] If

I took the maximum normally-advised course load of 36 credits in two semesters, the Introductory Psychology class would be 1/12th (3 credits out of 36 credits) of my total costs: $915 for the course, or $305 per credit.

If I took the route of distance learning, I might consider taking the course through University of Phoenix. The three-credit psychology course would cost me $1275, as each lower-division credit costs $410 plus approximately $15 in fees.[21] Thus my per-credit cost is $425.

Now, say I test out of the course using a CLEP exam and then transfer that test to one of the "Big Three" colleges of off-campus learning. The base per-credit cost of a CLEP test is as follows: the CLEP exam ($80) + the fee charged by the test center (around $30) = $110, divided by the number of credits earned (3 to 9, depending on the test) equals $12 to $37. The rest of the per-credit cost is enrollment, graduation, and other college fees. To limit enrollment costs when using this method, I would accumulate as many credits as I could before enrolling. To find the total cost of CLEP's Introductory Psychology exam, I divide the testing and enrollment costs at each college by the total number of credits earned. The CLEP per-credit cost is as follows:

Charter Oak State College: $222

Excelsior College: $275

Thomas Edison State University: $174[22]

CLEP Test Cost for Military Personnel and Veterans

Many military members qualify to have their first attempt at a CLEP test funded by the government through DANTES. Currently, members of the following are eligible: Air Force, Army, Marine Corps, Navy, Coast Guard, and National Guard & Reserve Component. Spouses and civil service civilian employees of the Air Force Reserve, Army Reserve, and Coast Guard are also eligible.[23] DANTES will fund both the exam fee and the administration fee if the test is taken at a base-sponsored test center but will fund only the exam fee if the test is taken at other test centers. Though only the first attempt of each test title is covered, test-takers can personally fund a retest after the three-month waiting period.

Veterans may also qualify to have their exam and administration fee funded through the GI Bill. Both of these fees are funded regardless of where you take the exam. You will need to apply for GI Bill benefits and then submit an application for reimbursement.[24]

IN A NUTSHELL

CLEP tests are an extremely practical and effective way to earn college credit. Without the need to enroll while you study, you can save thousands of dollars while you learn at your own pace using the materials you prefer. There are no residency costs to pay, no extension fees if you fall behind the schedule you set for yourself, and no frustrating concentration on information you already know. The price of these savings is the reduction of outside constraints to motivate and drive you. You become the director of one, which works well for some and terrible for others.

Even with the absence of mandated scheduling, there is nothing stopping you from setting yourself accountable to someone or something. Perhaps you have a family member or friend who will take on the role of accountability partner, or you reach out to a professional in your area. Technology's ability to assist our goals can hardly be overstated. Spreadsheets, electronic books, and productivity timers are just three of the learning accoutrements available. If you consider the internet, you have a plethora of ways to structure and motivate yourself, from educational podcasts to sample study schedules to online discussion forums.

Taking a CLEP test can seem daunting, especially when it's shrouded in unknowns and what-ifs. However, by breaking down the testing process into manageable steps and using the available CLEP resources (especially those online), CLEP testing becomes a straightforward and economical option for earning credit. CLEP tests launch you toward your goals while fostering habits of tenacity and self-motivation. Though test-taking has never been on my favorite activities list, and may not be on yours either, I encourage all to try this avenue for credit earning. The hardest part is getting started. Make it easier on yourself by finding the CLEP policy of the college you plan to attend, using practice tests to judge your readiness for the test, learning from others who have gone before you, and most importantly, getting yourself into the testing room.

TAKEAWAY TIPS

- Check your school's policy on CLEP tests. What are their guidelines for accepting credit?
- Don't hesitate to try a CLEP test to see if this learning method works for you.
- Visit the official website of your test for an overview of the test and to get you going in the right direction.
- Don't sweat the choice of your first test. A six-credit general exam is a good idea, as is a test in your favorite subject. If you like reading comprehension, try CLEP's Analyzing and Interpreting Literature worth three credits.
- Start with free resources and then check for reviews on test guides and textbooks before spending money.
- Use DegreeForum.net if you are stumped for an answer or need encouragement.
- Like exercise, the hardest part of credit-by-exam tests is getting started.

CHAPTER 5

MEET DSST TESTS

DSST tests are a type of credit-by-exam tests originally developed by the United States Department of Defense as a way for military members to earn credit while off campus, thus promoting a smooth transition from military service to the job market. DSST exams are administered through Prometric, a popular testing company owned by ETS (who also owns CLEP). Available for both military members and civilians, these exams are accepted at over 1,900 colleges and universities. If you are in the military, your first attempt of each DSST title is funded by the Defense Activity for Non-Traditional Educational Support (DANTES).[25]

Along with CLEP exams, DSST exams are often used as the groundwork of degrees earned off campus. However, because some DSST exams are worth upper-level credit, they can also be used to fill areas of a degree beyond those filled by CLEP. I used nine DSST exams in my bachelor's degree, and most of them fulfilled the upper-level credits in my social sciences concentration. When DSST exams are added to the equation, the students' credit-earning opportunities expand. To illustrate, let's return to our three student scenarios from the last chapter.

- Scenario one: You are a working toward becoming a registered nurse while earning an associate or bachelor's degree. You've used CLEP to fulfill general education requirements and free elective credits. Because you may now have reached the classes that are only offered online or have a lab requiring physical attendance, you may not see much help from DSST exams. However, DSST exams do add upper-level general education exams beyond the CLEP test repertoire, so do keep them in mind when planning your degree, especially if a CLEP test doesn't fit.
- Scenario two: You are an American history buff, and you have taken CLEP's History of the United States I and History of the United States II to earn six credits. You may be prepped to take DSST's The Civil War and Reconstruction (worth three credits) without any study. If you need to brush up on your Civil War facts, you will already have some background information because you've taken CLEP's U.S. History tests.
- Scenario three: You are a college-bound high school student with a few CLEP exams under your belt. If the college you plan to attend accepts them, you may want to add a DSST test or two. Your college likely publishes a list of accepted DSST tests and their corresponding course numbers on their website, which will enable you to determine which subject area each exam falls into (business, humanities, free electives, etc.) and which DSST tests are worth upper-level credit.[26]

DSST AND CLEP TEST COMPARISON

DSST tests are quite similar to CLEP tests, as both are computer-based, multiple choice, and pass/fail with no assigned grade. Also, both have a similar per-credit cost and are scored using points awarded for correct answers only, with no deduction for incorrect answers. DSST scores are shown at the end of the test, with the exception of the Principles of Public Speaking exam, which contains a speaking portion that is scored later. I have compiled a few facts about each program in the following table for comparison.

FEATURE:	CLEP	DSST
Test homepage:	http://clep.collegeboard.org/	http://getcollegecredit.com/
Test center search:	http://clep.collegeboard.org/search/test-centers	http://getcollegecredit.com/institutions/search/
Test titles and fact sheets:	http://clep.collegeboard.org/exam (Find your test and then follow links to view exam details, try sample questions, and see additional study resources.)	http://getcollegecredit.com/exam_fact_sheets (Find your exam and then click "Factsheet.")
Number of test titles:	33 (most worth lower-level credit)	34 (roughly ¾ of the tests are worth lower-level credit and ¼ are worth upper-level credit)
Test length:	90 minutes long (except the 120-minute College Composition test, and the 90-minute plus an optional 70-minute College Composition Modular test)	2 hours in length
How to send your score to the college of your choice on the day of the test:	CLEP uses two drop-down menus to allow you to select the state where the college is located and then select the name of the college itself. If you don't want to send your score for free at the time of the test (perhaps you don't know where you will be enrolling), first choose a state, and then select "Do not send" in the second drop-down box.	Before you go take an exam, you will need to use http://getcollegecredit.com/institutions/search/ to locate the four-digit code of the college where you would like your test score sent. You will be able to input your college's code when you register online before the test starts. If you don't wish to have your score sent for free on the day of the test, leave the four-digit code field blank.

FEATURE:	CLEP	DSST
Test scores kept on file:	For 20 years	Indefinitely
Cost to send test scores:	Free at time of test For accumulated scores to be sent to one college, $20 for civilians and $30 for military members. (The transcript for military members includes both CLEP and DSST scores.)	Free at time of test $30 for all accumulated DSST scores to be sent to one college. (There are two forms available for the military: one for a transcript of just DSST scores and one for a transcript of DSST and CLEP scores. Both transcripts cost $30 each.)
Transcript request form:	http://media.collegeboard.com/digitalServices/pdf/clep/clep-transcript-request-form.pdf Military members: http://getcollegecredit.com/images/uploads/documents/Military_DSST_CLEP_transcript_post74.pdf	http://getcollegecredit.com/test_takers Military members: To send solely DSST scores, use the link listed above. To send DSST and CLEP scores together: http://getcollegecredit.com/images/uploads/documents/Military_DSST_CLEP_transcript_post74.pdf

For a fascinating look at the scoring methods used for DSST tests, including the percentage of questions needed to pass each test, see this document online: http://getcollegecredit.com/assets/pdf/DSST_Exam_Scoring.pdf.

PREPARING FOR A DSST EXAM

Because DSST and CLEP are so alike, the preparatory steps for CLEP can be easily adapted to DSST with few changes. You may find it beneficial to refer to "CLEP Testing Step-by-Step" in chapter 4 as you prepare for a DSST test. The following is a collection of key DSST resources and sources for pretests. You can find more extensive information for some of these resources listed under CLEP's "Study Resources" and "Sources for Pretests" (steps 4 and 5).

Resources for DSST Tests

Alleydog.com (http://www.alleydog.com/): a website hosting a variety of material relating to psychology, including information compiled in class notes style. This information may be especially helpful for reviewing and memorizing specific tenants of psychology.

Amazon (http://www.amazon.com): an online e-commerce website. Out of all Amazon's qualities, I especially like their product reviews of study guides and books. These reviews, when taken with a grain of salt, are very informative. I found them useful to judge whether a textbook or study guide would be advantageous to my study and also to give me an idea of how difficult a text was.

DantesTestPrep (http://www.dantestestprep.com/): a website offering preparatory courses and free study guides for CLEP and DSST tests. I personally haven't used either of these, but the free guides seem to offer a convenient starting point for study or a concentrated review of test topics. The study guides also contain practice questions.

DSST Official Test Preparation Guide (http://www.collegetestprepguide.com/): a study guide covering the following ten exams: Criminal Justice, Ethics in America, Here's to Your Health, Introduction to Business, Introduction to World Religions, Management Information Systems, Personal Finance, Principles of Finance, Principles of Statistics, and Principles of Supervision. Of these ten titles, seven have been updated by DSST since the guide's publication, leaving Criminal Justice, Principles of Finance, and Principles of Supervision aligned with the current exams. While the guide is not created by the makers of DSST exams, it has been reviewed by Prometric, who develops DSST tests and states it is an accurate reflection of the actual test content. The guide costs $24.95 plus shipping, and is also available in electronic format; the whole electronic collection costs $24.95 and individual titles cost $9.95.

Finish College Fast (http://finishcollegefast.com/): study guides that cover 26 DSST tests. This resource is an option for those who want to broaden their pool of knowledge. Each course costs $35.97, so if you are on a budget, you may want to economize by using free resources first before branching out to priced resources like this one. DegreeForum.net has multiple reviews of these study guides.

Free-Clep-Prep (http://www.free-clep-prep.com/): a compilation of test preparation materials, most of which are free and available online. On the website, you will find free study guides for all of the DSST titles except Fundamentals of Cybersecurity. These study guides include information about each test, links to practice tests (some directly from Free-Clep-Prep and some from other websites), and study resource ideas. Once you've chosen a DSST title to pursue, look through the corresponding study guide for a learning jumpstart.

InstantCert (http://www.instantcert.com/): online flashcards for 29 of the 34 DSST titles. I highly recommend InstantCert flashcards for DSST tests. I studied their flashcards to complete Western Europe Since 1945, A History of the Vietnam War, An Introduction to the Modern Middle East, History of the Soviet Union, Organizational Behavior, Money and Banking, Substance Abuse, and The Civil War and Reconstruction. InstantCert's flashcards were the most accurate DSST resource I used.

Local Library: It is a good idea to visit your local library's website to see if they offer free DSST resources. Even layman's guides can help tremendously when you need a difficult topic explained. In addition to general college-related materials, look for a link to the "Testing & Education Reference Center."

McGraw-Hill Online Learning Center: resources that correspond to textbooks published by McGraw-Hill. Each textbook's learning center contains supplemental information like quizzes and flashcards. To find resources in the same topic as your exam, you can search the internet with the keywords "McGraw Hill HigherEd" and the name of your test subject.[27]

Official DSST Website (http://getcollegecredit.com): the official DSST website offering exam content outlines, sample questions, and a test center list. This is a great place to go for information when beginning a new DSST test.

Peterson's Official Guide to Mastering DSST Exams (http://www.petersonsbooks.com/categories/test-prep/dsst.html): the official DSST test preparation for the eight most-popular DSST exams. The guide offers diagnostic tests and posttests along with a review of each subject. The guide's materials for an individual subject can be downloaded separately in Kindle edition via Amazon.com. The eight exam titles are Business Mathematics, Ethics in America, Fundamentals of College Algebra, Introduction to Computing, Principles of Public Speaking, Principles of Supervision, Substance Abuse, and Technical Writing. For an in-depth preview of this test guide, see Amazon.com's "Look Inside" feature.

Peterson's Official Guide to Mastering DSST Exams (Part II) (http://www.petersonsbooks.com/categories/test-prep/dsst.html): a continuation of the above guide containing the following eight titles: The Civil War and Reconstruction, Environment and Humanity, Here's to Your Health, Human Resource Management, Introduction to Business, Introduction to World Religions, Organizational Behavior, and Personal Finance. This guide also includes diagnostic tests and posttests along with a subject review like the above guide.

Podcasts: audio (and sometimes video) files that provide another way to study. Podcasts for education are available through many providers and for various listening devices (computer, MP3 players, etc.). If you enjoy learning aurally, have lots of time in the car, or just want a change of pace, podcasts can be effective! If the situation allows, you may want to take notes while you listen. You can find podcasts online or from digital music providers.

Testing & Education Reference Center: contains free college and career information including study materials for DSST, CLEP, and other college tests. Peterson's practice tests are also available. You may be able to access this reference center through your library or, if you are enrolled, through your college. Military members have access as well. Please see CLEP's "Study Resources" in chapter 4 for more about how to access the center.

Textbooks: useful for unfamiliar topics or for a thorough introduction of subject. DSST's exam fact sheets include several textbooks that were used to develop the test content or are used at schools around the country to teach that particular subject. Even if you don't use the specific books mentioned, they can provide a handy comparison for other resources you are considering.

Wikipedia (http://www.wikipedia.org/): an online, collaborative encyclopedia. I relished having Wikipedia as a reference during my studies. Usually, I would go to Wikipedia to get more information about something that wasn't clear in the study guide or textbook I was using. Having access to this website saved me from banging my head against the wall on several occasions. Even though the typical Wikipedia content is far deeper than what is on a DSST test, just having access to another explanation can allow you to get through a difficult topic and move forward with your study. Sister site Wikibooks.org can also be used to find study books and texts.

Wise Owl Guides: study guides available through Amazon and Barnes & Noble. While researching study materials, I saw these guides mentioned on DegreeForum.net. I have not tried these guides, so the user reviews on DegreeForum.net and Amazon may help you decide if they are right for you.

The DSST resources I found most helpful were the Official DSST Practice tests, InstantCert, and Free-Clep-Prep.

My Favorite DSST Pretest Resources

DantesTestPrep (http://www.dantestestprep.com/): a company that primarily provides test preparation courses but also makes available free study guides and practice tests for 14 DSST titles. Each practice test contains 50 questions.

DSST Official Test Preparation Guide (http://www.collegetestprepguide. com/): a study guide covering the following ten exams, seven of which have been revised by DSST since this guide's publication. The three test titles that are still current are Criminal Justice, Principles of Finance, and Principles of Statistics. The guide contains practice tests with rationales.

Free-Clep-Prep (http://www.free-clep-prep.com/): free practice tests for 6 current DSST titles created by Justin Orgeron, the owner of the

Free-Clep-Prep. Since DSST practice exams are like hen's teeth, these exams are quite a treat. More importantly, the content of the practice tests is excellent preparation for the actual tests. Additional practice tests may be mentioned in the recommended resources listed for each test.

Official DSST Practice Tests (https://ibt.prometric.com/dsst): practice tests currently available for 22 titles. Some subjects have two practice tests available. Each test costs $5 ($10 for Fundamentals of Cybersecurity), and the number of test questions varies (for example, the Money and Banking practice test contained 35 questions). However, because the practice tests are created by DSST, you will find the practice tests' questions and format to be extremely similar to the real exam.

To take a practice test, you will need to create an account with Prometric (which develops and administers DSST tests and practice tests). This account is separate from the account you will use to take the actual test. Thus, it can be helpful to put "practice test" or "PT" in the username of the account you use when taking practice tests to help keep the two accounts straight.

Peterson's Official Guide to Mastering DSST Exams (http://www. petersonsbooks.com/categories/test-prep/dsst.html): the official DSST test preparation for the eight most-popular DSST exams: Business Mathematics, Ethics in America, Fundamentals of College Algebra, Introduction to Computing, Principles of Public Speaking, Principles of Supervision, Substance Abuse, and Technical Writing. The guide includes a 20-question diagnostic test that helps you gauge your knowledge and a 60-question posttest that will show how prepared you are for the actual test.

Peterson's Official Guide to Mastering DSST Exams (Part II) (http:// www.petersonsbooks.com/categories/test-prep/dsst.html): a continuation of the above guide containing the following eight titles: The Civil War and Reconstruction, Environment and Humanity, Here's to Your Health, Human Resource Management, Introduction to Business, Introduction to World Religions, Organizational Behavior, and Personal Finance. This guide is identical in format to Peterson's first official guide: 20 diagnostic questions with 60 post-study questions for each subject.

Peterson's Practice Tests (http://www.petersons.com/college-search/

dsst-practice-test.aspx): full-length practice tests for 21 titles. Because DSST practice tests seem to be harder to find than CLEP practice tests, these tests are very handy when preparing to take a DSST exam. Military members can take these tests for free by signing in at the following website: http://www.nelnetsolutions.com/dod/. Civilians can take these tests for free, too, via the Testing & Education Reference Center (see "Study Resources" for CLEP in chapter 4 for details). Otherwise, the practice tests cost $19.95 apiece and can be accessed through Peterson's website.

Recommendations for other helpful resources can be located on DegreeForum. net, both in the general area of the forum and the Specific Exam Feedback section.
On page 192 you'll find my DSST test reviews that list the textbooks and other materials I used to prepare for ten test titles.

TAKEAWAY TIPS

- Examine your college's DSST test policies, including which tests are accepted and how they apply to a degree.
- DSST exams can be a great way to add upper-level credits to your degree plan through credit-by-exam.
- Utilize the content outlines and suggested resources from the official DSST website.
- DSST test materials can be harder to find than CLEP materials. You may be able to source materials through companies that offer CLEP test resources and through the internet.

CHAPTER 6

SPECIALIZED LEARNING METHODS

Now that you have been introduced to CLEP and DSST exams, you are ready to learn about other credit-earning opportunities that are available. I've included the word *specialized* in the title of this chapter because these off-campus credit methods tend to be usable in degrees that either have been specifically set up to accommodate these methods or have the flexibility to include one or more of these methods. This means you may only be able to apply these techniques to a particular degree plan, or you may have to earn your credits through one school/company and then transfer them to another. However, just because these programs are more specialized doesn't mean they are ineffective. Use the following companies, exams, and programs to match credit-earning options with the knowledge you already have or wish to gain.

A Word about Cost

Knowing what to pay for academic resources can be tricky. You can find nearly every level of educational information at virtually any price. Because there are so many excellent free resources, it's a good idea to use discretion when purchasing study materials. Websites like YouTube and Khan Academy, along with massive open online courses (MOOCs) and internet forums may give you enough gratis resources to carry you through your entire preparation for a course or exam.

However, just because there is a multitude of free resources is no reason to eschew priced resources. During my degree journey, I struggled with finding a balance when it came to purchasing resources, especially those online. For example, I sometimes hesitated to buy practice tests that weren't free, even though practice tests were a fundamental part of my study routine and I had budgeted money for them. I realize now that between the educational return on your investment and the time saved by not having to hunt for just the right free resource, paid resources can easily be worth their cost. If you're thinking about giving a paid resource a try, it's advantageous to look for reviews (especially on DegreeForum.net) to find out if the service is effective and relevant.

Credit Recommendations

First, what are credit recommendations? There are two companies that review courses and certifications in order to provide colleges with a recommendation of how many credits a certain course or certification is worth. Colleges can then use these recommendations when creating their own policy toward accepting those courses or certifications. A course that has been reviewed for credit is appropriately designated a credit-recommended course.

One of the two companies offering recommendations is the American Council on Education (http://www.acenet.edu). The ACE is involved in representing higher education at the federal level, in assisting adult learners and non-traditional students, and in promoting research in education worldwide. The ACE's College Credit Recommendation Service (CREDIT) is dedicated to reviewing courses and certifications earned "outside traditional degree programs" and to offering a recommendation as to how many college credits each is worth.[28] The ACE has reviewed over 35,000 courses. You can visit ACE's website to view their catalog of courses, which are grouped by test provider.[29]

While ACE's CREDIT is the more well-known and far-reaching credit recommendation service, the other credit-recommending program is the National College Credit Recommendation Service (NCCRS- http://www. nationalccrs.org/). Conducted by the New York State Board of Regents, the NCCRS functions in the same capacity as ACE's CREDIT. The NCCRS has reviewed and recommended for credit approximately 5,200 courses and educational programs. These courses can be found in the College Credit Recommendations Directory.[30]

When selecting a college course or exam to pursue for credit, it is important to check if it carries any credit recommendations. You will need to verify that the course's recommendation type is accepted at the college where you are going to transfer your course. Let's use a CLEP test as an example. First we visit ACE's website and browse the organizations to locate "College Board's College-Level Examination Program (CLEP)." After clicking on the organization's link, we find that all 33 of CLEP's offerings have received credit recommendations from ACE.

Next, we visit the website of the college where we plan to transfer our credit, say, Liberty University. We navigate to the area of their website that deals with transferring credit and shows the types of credit they accept.[31] CLEP tests are listed here. Following the link to learn more about CLEP, we see that Liberty University awards credit for all 33 CLEP tests.

What about other lesser-known courses/tests, such as the ones detailed in this chapter? Continuing with our Liberty University example, courses/tests with ACE or NCCRS credit recommendations are considered by the university, meaning they may be eligible for credit in accordance with the university's policy. Sometimes you can find this policy listed on the website (as with our CLEP test example), or you may need to ask the college directly about a certain course/test to find out if it's accepted and how many credits it's worth.

Liberty University's method of handling transfer credit is very common. The big-name tests, such as CLEP, will generally transfer, as will courses that have been reviewed by ACE or NCCRS. Other types of credit will vary in transfer rate, and often a course without a credit recommendation from ACE or NCCRS will not be given credit at a college or university. Thus, I suggest caution, but not avoidance, when pursuing the specialized learning methods described in this chapter. I've seen many posts regarding this topic on DegreeForum.net—posts where students lament the fact that a specialized course didn't transfer as they had hoped, and posts from DegreeForum.

net regulars filled with reminders to check before completing a course that it will be accepted at the receiving college. Conducting a little research will save you both time and money.

SPECIALIZED LEARNING METHOD LIST

ALEKS: http://www.aleks.com/

ALEKS (Assessment and LEarning in Knowledge Spaces) is an online program designed to enhance your education by customizing the study material to what you need to learn. The program first tests you on the subject of your choice using the "ALEKS Assessment" to determine in which area(s) of the subject you need practice. Next, you move into the "Learning Mode," where you learn several topics that are appropriate for your knowledge of the subject. Periodically, the program will assess your overall mastery of the subject. Once you reach 70% or more on this mastery assessment, you will have completed the course.

While ALEKS offers courses for students in kindergarten through college, nine of their higher education courses have been reviewed by ACE and given credit recommendations. Receiving credit for these courses is outlined at the following page: http://www.aleks.com/about_aleks/ace_credit. The process includes visiting the ACE transcript website and transferring your ALEKS course to your ACE transcript using their outlined procedure.[32] The courses are given a pass/fail designation rather than a letter grade.

ALEKS is available as a monthly, 6-month, or 12-month subscription plan. The cost for each plan is $19.95, $99.95, and $179.95, respectively. There is a family discount for multiple students if you choose the 6- or 12-month plan. Each student is allowed to work on only one course at a time, but the student can change to another course at any time with no extra charge. To gain credit for a completed course before switching to a new course, make sure that ALEKS displays the message that the course has been approved and submitted to ACE for processing.

Community College Courses:

Another way to earn credit for a low per-credit cost is through a community college. Often, these colleges provide inexpensive hands-on instruction in courses that aren't as well suited to off-campus learning. When compared to four-year institutions, community colleges usually have lower student-teacher ratios, which allow the community college to offer more personalization to students.

A major downside to community college is that most state and private four-year colleges/universities put a cap on the number of community college credits you can transfer. At the Big Three, the limit of credits that can be transferred from accredited community colleges is as follows: Charter Oak State College, 87; Excelsior College, 105; Thomas Edison State University, 80.[33] While these three colleges accept a large number of community college credits, other colleges and universities aren't so generous. Sometimes you can bypass these credit limits by earning a degree from the community college where you acquired the credit. You may then be able to transfer your degree, rather than your credits, and gain access to higher levels of learning at another college or university. Other drawbacks of community colleges are that you may need to go on campus for at least part of the class and that the schedule for a community college course can be less flexible than a credit-by-exam course.

Community college classes find their purpose in the off-campus learner's portfolio of resources as a way to earn credits for a change of pace, to take a hands-on course locally, or to best fulfill certain needs (see Frederick Community College within the FEMA Independent Study Program section below). Also, community colleges can allow you to earn your degree economically yet still maintain some flexibility in your overall degree completion timeline.

FEMA Independent Study Program: http://training.fema.gov/IS/

To fulfill 16 of my 27 free elective credits, I completed online FEMA courses. These free classes, which are taken at your own pace, teach a variety of subjects centering on emergency preparedness. I learned useful information about how an emergency is handled by local, state, and federal employees; how I personally can be prepared for emergencies; and which hazards are greatest for my home county. There was enough diversity in the course offerings that I was able to choose those that were both enriching and appealing. A course titled Introduction to Residential Coastal Construction, with emphasis on mitigation of environmental hazards, was especially fascinating because I love the coast and hope to own a coastal property someday.

Most courses only require achieving a set percentage on the final exam, while a few courses have short requisite quizzes throughout the course. There are no fees, and you can retake the exam if you do not score high enough to pass. For rounding out an already challenging degree plan, FEMAs can be an answer to prayer. They are also a great way to save money for the more expensive aspects of a degree.

Before beginning a FEMA course, check with your college to determine if they accept FEMA credits, and if they do, find out which courses are worth college credit, as not all of FEMA's offerings are. While some of FEMA's on-campus Emergency Management Institute courses have ACE credit recommendations, currently none of FEMA's Independent Study courses have ACE credit recommendations.[34] This does reduce the likelihood that these courses will be accepted "raw," that is, accepted by sending your FEMA transcript directly to a college. One school that accepts raw FEMA credits is Charter Oak State College.

Some colleges will accept FEMA credits only if they are on a transcript from another college. Excelsior College is one of these colleges. To get credit at a college with this policy, first enroll at a college that does grant credit for raw FEMA credit. For clarity, let's call this intermediary college "College Z." After sending your FEMA course transcript to College Z, you have your FEMA courses put on your College Z transcript by following the required steps (such as paying for the credits and having a transcript created). Then, you send this transcript to your primary college to be applied to your degree. A popular intermediary college is Frederick Community College, which has a dedicated program for FEMA credit transfer.[35]

While I was able to use FEMA courses to earn over half of my free elective credits toward my BA in Social Sciences from Thomas Edison State University, FEMA credits are no longer accepted at TESU, raw or otherwise.[36] I mention this to bring attention to the ever-changing nature of the college landscape and as a reminder to keep an eye out for changes and new opportunities when using FEMA courses to earn credit.

Since earning credit for FEMA courses varies from college to college, it is crucial to explore your school's FEMA policy before taking FEMA courses. For an overview of the FEMA course process, see Justin Orgeron's FEMA Course page at Free-Clep-Prep.com (http://www.free-clep-prep.com/FEMA-Courses.html).

Foreign Language Proficiency Tests:

Until I wrote this chapter, I had no idea that so many language tests existed! The Spanish language CLEP test covered my foreign language skills, so I didn't pursue more advanced tests. However, if you are bilingual or if you enjoy learning languages as a hobby, these tests may help you earn credit for those skills. For ease in comparability, I've compiled information on a few popular standardized language tests in table format below.

AMERICAN COUNCIL ON THE TEACHING OF FOREIGN LANGUAGES (ACTFL) ORAL PROFICIENCY INTERVIEW (OPI)		
Note: There are other tests available from ACTFL that assess skills other than speaking.[37]		
http://www.languagetesting.com/		
LANGUAGES AVAILABLE:	**SKILLS TESTED:**	**CREDITS:**
Afrikaans, Akan-Twi, Albanian, Amharic, Arabic, Armenian, Azerbaijani, Bengali, Bosnian, Bulgarian, Burmese, Cambodian, Cantonese, Cebuano, Chavacano, Chinese-Mandarin, Czech, Dari, Dutch, English, French, Ga, Georgian, German, Greek (Modern), Gujarati, Haitian Creole, Hausa, Hebrew, Hiligaynon, Hindi, Hmong-Mong, Hungarian, Igbo, Ilocano, Indonesian, Italian, Japanese, Javanese, Kashmiri, Kazakh, Kikongo-Kongo, Korean, Krio, Kurdish, Lao, Malay, Malayalam, Mandingo-Bambara, Nepali, Pashto, Persian-Farsi, Polish, Portuguese, Punjabi, Romanian, Russian, Serbian/Croatian, Sindhi, Sinhalese, Slovak, Somali, Spanish, Swahili, Swedish, Tagalog, Tajik, Tamil, Tausug, Telugu, Thai, Turkish, Turkmen, Uighur, Ukrainian, Urdu, Uzbek, Vietnamese, Wolof, Yoruba	Speaking only	ACE recommends: up to 6 lower-level and 6 upper-level[38]

AP COURSES

Note: These tests are designed for high school students and are only offered once per year.

https://apstudent.collegeboard.org

LANGUAGES AVAILABLE:	SKILLS TESTED:	CREDITS:
Chinese Language and Culture, French Language and Culture, German Language and Culture, Italian Language and Culture, Japanese Language and Culture, Latin, Spanish Language and Culture, Spanish Literature and Culture	All Language and Culture exams: listening, reading, writing, and speaking. Latin: reading and comprehending, translating, contextualizing, and analyzing poetry and prose. Spanish Literature and Culture: listening, reading, and writing.	ACE recommends: 3-16 lower-level[39]

BRIGHAM YOUNG UNIVERSITY (BYU) FOREIGN LANGUAGE ACHIEVEMENT TESTING SERVICE (FLATS)

http://flats.byu.edu/

LANGUAGES AVAILABLE:	SKILLS TESTED:	CREDITS:
Albanian, Arabic, Armenian, Bulgarian, Cambodian, Cantonese-Simplified, Cantonese-Traditional, Cebuano, Croatian, Czech, Danish, Dutch, Estonian, Fijian, Finnish, French, Georgian, German, Greek, Haitian-Creole, Hmong, Hungarian, Icelandic, Ilonggo-Hiligaynon, Indonesian, Italian, Japanese, Korean, Latvian, Lithuanian, Malagasy, Malay, Mandarin-Simplified, Mandarin-Traditional, Mongolian, Norwegian, Persian-Farsi, Polish, Portuguese-Brazilian, Portuguese-Continental, Romanian, Russian, Samoan, Serbian, Spanish, Swedish, Tagalog, Tahitian, Thai, Tongan, Ukrainian, Vietnamese	Listening, reading, and grammar comprehension questions in multiple-choice format[40]	No credit recommendation from ACE or NCCRS. BYU is accredited by the Northwest Commission on Colleges and Universities. Usually 12 to 16 lower-level[41]

CLEP

http://clep.collegeboard.org/exam

LANGUAGES AVAILABLE:	SKILLS TESTED:	CREDITS:
French, German, Spanish	Understanding spoken & written language	ACE recommends: 6 or 9 lower-level[42]

NEW YORK UNIVERSITY (NYU) FOREIGN LANGUAGE PROFICIENCY EXAM

https://www.scps.nyu.edu/academics/departments/foreign-languages/testing.html

LANGUAGES AVAILABLE:	SKILLS TESTED:	CREDITS:
Afrikaans, Albanian, Arabic, Armenian, Bengali, Bosnian, Bulgarian, Cantonese, Catalan, Chinese, Croatian, Czech, Danish, Dutch, Finnish, French, German, Greek (Modern), Gujarati, Haitian Creole, Hebrew, Hindi, Hungarian, Ibo, Icelandic, Indonesian, Irish, Italian, Japanese, Korean, Latin, Lithuanian, Malay, Mandarin, Norwegian, Persian, Polish, Portuguese (Brazilian), Punjabi, Romanian, Russian, Serbian, Spanish, Swahili, Swedish, Tagalog, Thai, Turkish, Ukrainian, Urdu, Vietnamese, Yiddish, Yoruba	Listening, reading, and writing Optional 350-word essay (worth 4 credits)	No credit recommendation from ACE or NCCRS. NYU is accredited by the Middle States Commission on Higher Education. Up to 16 at COSC and TESU[43]

OHIO UNIVERSITY COURSE CREDIT BY EXAMINATION (CCE)		
https://www.ohio.edu/ecampus/print/course-list.html#course-credit		
LANGUAGES AVAILABLE:	**SKILLS TESTED:**	**CREDITS:**
Elementary French I, Elementary French II, Intermediate French I, Intermediate French II, Elementary Spanish I, Elementary Spanish II, Intermediate Spanish I, Intermediate Spanish II	Elementary French I and II: grammar, listening, speaking, vocabulary, and writing skills Intermediate French I and II: grammar, reading, vocabulary, and writing Spanish courses: grammar, reading, vocabulary, and writing	No credit recommendation from ACE or NCCRS. Ohio University is accredited by the Higher Learning Commission. 4 lower-level for each elementary exam and 3 lower-level for each intermediate exam at Ohio University.[44]

LearningCounts: https://learningcounts.org/

LearningCounts provides colleges with a prior learning assessment program that allows students to create portfolios for credit. LearningCounts is partnered with select universities, corporations, and colleges (including Excelsior College and Thomas Edison State University), and these institutions have specific policies in place on how they will accept credits earned using LearningCounts' services.

To begin the portfolio process, students contact one of the 50+ partner schools to enroll in a LearningCounts' portfolio development course. This course walks learners through the process of identifying, compiling, and documenting their college-level learning. The cost of this course is set by the college.[45]

What advantage does LearningCounts offer an off-campus student? It depends on the type of experiences you are documenting and how much it costs to complete the program. There is no guarantee of earning credit when LearningCounts reviews your portfolio, and students will need to discuss program costs with the individual colleges. Combat these uncertainties by doing research before you enroll. Learn what types of knowledge and experience are best suited to prior learning assessment.[46] Each portfolio corresponds to one undergraduate college course, and the average number of credits earned through portfolios is nine.[47]

Are the breadth and depth of your subject matter worth the time and money necessary to compile portfolios, or would it be easier to demonstrate your knowledge through credit-by-exam tests? Though prior learning assessment can require more work to get started, your portfolio credit can accumulate quickly once you learn the routine.

PLA testing through LearningCounts is on the list of approved tests for reimbursement under the GI Bill.[48]

Massive Open Online Course (MOOC):

A MOOC is a widely accessible course available online and usually offered for free. Most MOOCs are created by colleges and universities, and their topics stretch from computer science to philosophy to music composition. The formality of MOOCs ranges from a completely student-controlled course using freely available lectures to an on-campus-style, professor-directed course with an enrollment period, class-size limits, and required student participation. MOOCs offer students a large degree of flexibility in their education because of easy enrollment, online access, and the ability to choose their level of commitment.

A few popular MOOC providers are Udacity (https://www.udacity.com/), Coursera (https://www.coursera.org/), edX (https://www.edx.org/), and Udemy (https://www.udemy.com/), though there are many, many others! MOOC's Wikipedia page (https://en.wikipedia.org/wiki/MOOC) has a partial listing of other companies within the "Notable providers" section. Because there are so many individual websites offering MOOCs, there are other websites that exist strictly to categorize the available MOOCs. Here are a few examples of MOOC aggregators: the Open Education Consortium (http://www.oeconsortium.org/courses/), MOOC List (http://www.mooc-list.com/), and My Education Path (http://myeducationpath.com/courses/).

Gaining college credit by completing MOOCs is a hot-button issue and a topic worthy of continued discussion. At present, only a select number of MOOCs are granted college credit at participating colleges. To bridge the credit gap, degree-seeking students can capitalize on MOOCs for their free resources while earning credit through other methods. Credit-by-exam tests pair especially well with MOOCs. When lining up resources for an upcoming test, browsing a MOOC aggregator for relevant courses is an excellent habit.

Military Experience:

ACE has reviewed many of the military's courses/occupations and given credit recommendations. On the ACE College Credit for Military Service page, you will find links to the Military Guide; Transcripts for Military Personnel; and Transfer Guide: Understanding Your Military Transcript and ACE Credit Recommendations.[49] The ACE Military Guide offers two search features which enable users to locate their course or occupation for credit information. As with all ACE recommendations, the burden of substantiating those credits rests with the individual college/university.

The Army, Coast Guard, Marine Corps, National Guard, and Navy use the Joint Services Transcript for all educational courses completed.[50] Air Force members will receive a transcript from the Community College of the Air Force (CCAF).[51] Military students interested in earning college credit will need to send their transcript to the college of their choice for review. You may even choose to do this before enrolling, as some colleges will give you an evaluation of your credits before you enroll. This usually costs $100, although sometimes it's free. At Thomas Edison State University, you can use your Joint Services Transcript to receive a free, pre-enrollment evaluation. Details can be found here: https://mvp.tesu.edu/.

If you can't find information about the type of credit you are transferring by contacting the college and searching DegreeForum.net and other websites, or if your credits are unique in some way, the evaluation may be a wise use of money. Otherwise, you can wait to send your transcripts until you apply.

NFA (National Fire Academy): http://www.usfa.fema.gov/nfa/

The National Fire Academy courses are very similar in structure and purpose to FEMA courses. NFA and FEMA courses are designed for emergency services personnel (but available to all civilians), and their online courses are free. Unlike FEMA courses, some of the NFA's courses have been given credit recommendations by the ACE. To find courses that have ACE recommendations, visit the National Guide to College Credit for Workforce Training section of ACE website at http://www2.acenet.edu/credit/ and navigate to the "National Emergency Training Center (NFA)."[52] The courses that begin with Q are those offered online. As with FEMA courses, check with your college to determine which courses are accepted for credit before you begin. When you are ready to transfer your completed NFA courses to your school, use ACE's credit transcript service.

Penn Foster College: http://www.pennfoster.edu/college

Penn Foster is one name you may see when perusing DegreeForum.net, mainly in discussions of online college courses with a low per-credit cost ($79) and ACE credit recommendations. Penn Foster can be a viable option if you have taken as many CLEP/DSST tests as your college will accept, or if Penn Foster offers a subject not covered by other exams. Visit Penn Foster's Individual College Course page for a list of courses you can take without enrolling: http://www.pennfoster.edu/college/all-programs/college-courses. When selecting a Penn Foster course to pursue, be sure to verify the course's ACE credit recommendation and that the course is current by visiting ACE's credit website, clicking on the title of the course, and viewing the dates offered, as both the ACE recommendations and the course offerings are updated periodically.[53]

Portfolio Assessment:

Judging by Brad Voeller's experience related in his book, *Accelerated Distance Learning*, Thomas Edison State University's Portfolio Development used to be a fast and germane way to earn credit. Today, portfolio development at TESU has evolved to be one of the more cumbersome ways to earn credit, partly due to the mandatory 12-week time frame of the PLA preparatory courses (unless you use the free, non-credit open course versions) and the costs similar to those of an online class. Its ultimate drawback is not knowing whether you will receive credit for your experiences until you finish the course. Thus, you may work through the labor-intensive process and walk away with three credits for completing the course and no credit for your experiences.[54]

Nevertheless, the essence of the portfolio program is highly compatible with the goals of most off-campus learners, so if you think you might benefit from creating a portfolio, use TESU's website to check the current portfolio requirements and process.[55] Also, read what other portfolio users are saying online. These two strategies will help you determine if portfolio development is suited to the type of experiences for which you are seeking credit.

While I use the portfolio program at TESU as my example above, other colleges offer a similar way to gain credit for life experiences. Excelsior College, Charter Oak, and Kaplan University all have portfolio processes comparable to TESU in that the student works through a course to introduce the portfolio process and is then eligible to compile and submit proof of college-level learning.[56]

The portfolio program's strengths lie in offering credit for relatively obscure or unique certifications and experiences. Credit for more common subjects can be awarded less expensively and more efficiently through CLEP, DSST, and other standard credit-by-exam tests.

See FAQs for Chapter 6 for other details about TESU's PLA process.

Saylor Academy: http://www.saylor.org/

In an easy-to-navigate and beautifully laid out web format, Saylor Academy has created a place for students to learn free of charge with the opportunity to gain credit for what they have learned. Saylor Academy is a helpful place for off-campus learners to find preparatory resources for CLEP, DSST, TECEP, UExcel, StraighterLine and other tests and to earn credit directly from the academy. The company is taking steps to offer more courses and currently has seven ACE-evaluated courses and nine NCCRS-reviewed courses.

On the Third Party College Credit Options page (http://www.saylor.org/credit/third-party-credit-exams/), you will find Saylor Academy courses directly matched with specific test titles from other companies. Generally, to earn credit once you have determined that your school will accept a certain exam or Saylor Academy course and you have finished studying the course, the next step is to take the corresponding final exam, whether that be a CLEP, TECEP, or the final exam from Saylor Academy. You can then transfer your CLEP credits, your TESU transcript, or your Saylor Academy transcript to your college.

StraighterLine: http://www.straighterline.com/

Founded in 2009, StraighterLine seeks to cut costs for students by stream-lining the sequence of earning college credit. The company offers in-house courses at the college level that have been given credit recommendations by the American Council on Education (ACE). Acceptance of StraighterLine courses varies from college to college, but the ACE recommendation does make StraighterLine credit more widely transferable. Charter Oak State College, Excelsior College, and Thomas Edison State University are partner colleges with StraighterLine, meaning they grant full credit for Straighter-Line's courses that apply to the student's degree plan. Currently, Straighter-Line has 99 partner colleges.

StraighterLine's website can be used to match a StraighterLine course with its equivalent course at one of their partner colleges. These very use-ful lists of equivalencies can be found by visiting StraighterLine.com, navi-gating to the partner college of interest, and clicking "Course Equivalency."

Pricing for StraighterLine is $99/month for membership plus a $49 typical fee per course. StraighterLine also offers a free personalized degree plan to help you apply their courses to a degree plan from one of their partner colleges.[57]

TECEP (Thomas Edison Credit by Exam Program) Exams: http://www.tesu.edu/degree-completion/Testing.cfm

TECEP exams are Thomas Edison State University's own brand of credit-by-exam test. Although I didn't take any of these exams to earn my degree, my sister completed seven. The 33 exams presently available cover a broad range of subjects in both upper- and lower-level credit. The upper-level ex-ams can be especially useful when completing a TESU degree complete-ly off campus. TECEP exams can also be transferred to Charter Oak State College, Excelsior College, and other colleges in the same manner as credit earned on campus at TESU.[58]

To better compare TECEP exams with other credit-by-exam methods, I've calculated the approximate per-credit cost of TECEP exams. Depending on the tuition plan used and how many TECEP exams verses online cours-es you take from TESU, the per-credit cost varies from $109 to $174.[59] This includes tuition and enrollment expenses for earning a degree from TESU; applying TECEP exam credit to a degree from another college will affect the per-credit cost.

There are three ways to take a TECEP exam: at the university in Trenton, New Jersey; online using ProctorU (the college's online proctor service); or at a local public library or accredited college/university. For the local options, you will need to arrange for a full-time librarian or a college testing center employee to proctor your exam, following the guidelines on TESU's website.[60] The librarian or testing center staff member will need to fill out a proctor request form that TESU will review for approval. The ProctorU method allows you to take the exam online; the other two methods are administered using pen and paper.

In regard to the difficulty of TECEPs, every person I've encountered (including my sister) who has taken and compared a TECEP test and a CLEP test said that the TECEP test was more difficult. This is not surprising since the majority of TECEP tests are upper-level, and CLEP tests are almost always lower-level. However, TECEP tests are easier in the regard of having a specific textbook to study. For a CLEP test, your study materials are usually more varied and broad, while with a TECEP test, everything you need to know for the test is contained in the recommended textbook(s).

My sister felt this difference almost immediately. After studying a few days for her first TECEP exam, she remarked, "A TECEP exam is more like an on-campus college class where you read and study one or two textbooks to prepare for the final exam." On TESU's website, you can view each test's course outline, which lists recommended textbooks and practice problems (you do not need to be enrolled or signed up for a TECEP exam to view any of the outlines).[61]

TECEP tests have increased in popularity in the last few years, thanks to Thomas Edison State University's reduction of the exam price in 2011. With a per-credit price comparable to a typical CLEP or DSST test and credit that can be transferred to other colleges as easily as credit earned on campus, these exams can be a natural next step after CLEP and DSST tests to add upper-level credit to your degree plan through credit-by-exam.

TEEX (Texas A&M Engineering Extension Service) courses: http://teex.org/

These online Texas A&M courses are offered for free, as they are funded by DHS/FEMA. Ten of these online courses have been given credit recommendations by the ACE; all ten are in the subject area of cybersecurity. To find these ten, view the TEEX website and navigate to the cybersecurity section of courses. One way to locate these courses is by searching the TEEX website using the phrase "Information Technology / Online Training" (including the spaces around the slash).[62] The ten courses are divided into three tracks:

- CYB101: Cybersecurity for Everyone—Non-Technical
- CYB201: Cybersecurity for IT Professionals—Technical
- CYB301: Cybersecurity for Business Professionals—Business Managers

Each track is recommended to be worth two credits, and the tracks do not duplicate each other, meaning you can earn a total of six college credits.[63]

UExcel Exams (formerly known as Excelsior College Examinations or ECEs): http://www.excelsior.edu/exams/uexcel-home

UExcel exams are credit-by-exam tests created by Excelsior College. There are currently 55 UExcel exams—some worth lower-level credit and some worth upper-level credit. These exams are another way to earn that often elusive upper-level credit while off campus. In terms of difficulty, test-takers report that these are some of the more challenging credit-by-exam tests. If you have become familiar with the typical credit-by-exam testing method and have developed study strategies that suit your learning style, there's no need to be afraid to dive into these exams. These exams are accepted at the other Big Three schools, and there are numerous other colleges that accept UExcel exams because the exams have been recommended for credit by the ACE.[64]

UExcel exams are administered at Pearson VUE Test Centers. A list of these centers is available at http://www.pearsonvue.com/uexcel/. The cost for a 3-credit lower-level undergraduate UExcel exam is typically $95.[65] Enrollment at Excelsior is not required.

Excelsior's UExcel website (above) has a wonderful walkthrough of the process of taking a UExcel exam, and it has a downloadable Content Guide for each exam that includes a study resource list (other resources can be sourced from DegreeForum.net) and sample questions with rationales. A practice test is also available for many of the exams. InstantCert offers flashcards for 11 UExcel exams; see the InstantCert homepage for a list of available titles.

Using Specialized Credit Methods

Though I've mentioned only a few of the numerous ways to earn credit, you can take the principles of this chapter and apply them to other credit-earning opportunities you find. Using courses or exams with ACE or NCCRS credit recommendations increases the likelihood that you will be able to transfer your credit to the college of your choice. However, regardless of the credit recommendations of a course or exam you are considering, be sure to check with the college where you plan to transfer the credit, as each college sets its own policies and has complete control over which credit it accepts. It's also a good idea to look for information from other students who have previously used a certain program or exam. With these two points in mind, you can use specialized learning methods to expand your credit-earning avenues tremendously.

TAKEAWAY TIPS

- When it comes to buying college textbooks and online resources, it is worth the time to research your options. User reviews can be very helpful.
- Before pursuing a new type of test or course, look into its credit recommendation.
- Visit the website of the college where you want to transfer your credits to find which tests and courses they accept.
- Excelsior College has a handy PDF entitled "A Guide to Open Educational Resources (OER)," that contains links to different courses and study materials: http://www.excelsior.edu/exams/open-educational-resources.

CHAPTER 7

MOTIVATION

don't know how you do it."

Thinking about this phrase brings to mind conversations between acquaintances and me about getting a college degree off campus. The phrase summarizes their responses. Even in our age of digital information, pursuing a college degree has strongly attached connotations and assumptions. For the student, this includes leaving home and being taught by a professor in a classroom. Since I diverged from this typical path, others may find it hard to envision the off-campus journey I took, let alone visualize taking that journey themselves.

So, how did I do it? How did I, and how do other students like me, earn an accredited degree for $10,000? Since this entire book is my long answer to this question, let's move to the next questions: How did I stay motivated and keep on track? Where did I go to get help? These two questions are topics for the next two chapters.

How does a student complete the process of starting, learning, adapting, growing, and finishing strong? Specific test preparation methods and insider credit opportunities aside, succeeding on the off-campus path boils down to drive and tenacity. Drive and tenacity stem from at least one reason why the student wants to earn a degree off campus. This reason is the motivator.

MY MOTIVATING FACTORS

I needed more than one reason to complete college non-traditionally. Having several clear goals would thwart inclinations to throw in the towel. I began college in September of 2008 with the three educational goals of acquiring knowledge, helping my family, and using my time wisely. Over the course of my degree, I incorporated these basic ideas into what became my four motivating factors of college: glorify God, save money, live at home, and earn my bachelor's degree.

Since I am a Christian, I wanted my higher education choices to reflect my commitment to following biblical principles. There was nothing stopping me from taking these principles with me to a college campus, but from what I had observed and discovered first-hand, I could more easily fulfill my commitment and my degree if I remained off campus. Using money frugally, avoiding social drama, maintaining a focus on study, and personalizing my education were all improved for me by being off campus. I was able to tailor my curriculum to not just my learning style and personal taste but to include religious studies, Creationism alongside Darwinism, and Christian-specific methods of counseling.

Curriculum was a big motivator, but so was money. When I graduated from high school, I had a choice: go on campus and almost certainly walk away with student debt along with my diploma, or study off campus and pay cash for my degree. This was a simple decision. To be sure, not all cases are this simple, such as when a student chooses a degree not well-suited to off-campus learning or if the student's college does not accommodate off-campus study methods. However, for the increasing number of students able to take advantage of off-campus credit, the monetary savings can give those individuals a life-altering freedom: liberation from student debt. Avoiding debt requires conscientious effort, but once you make it a priority, you will find ways to keep your goal. Some of the ways I saved money were minor adjustments, such as buying used textbooks; other ways were major lifestyle commitments, such as living at home.

Of my four motivating factors, living at home is probably the most controversial. How would I continue to learn and gain new experiences if I remained at home? Isn't socialization one of the pillars of the college experience? While most of us can agree that college does help students mature and make social connections, our differing opinions relate to what extent this maturation and socialization occur exclusively on campus. However, in spite of these opinions, we can all agree that different people thrive in different environments. Our social setting plays a large role in encouraging our study habits, attitudes, and certainly our moods. Having the ability to choose a setting where I would be most productive and consistent is why my study location was one of my motivating factors. Selecting this environment requires self-knowledge. Fortunately, by the time most students reach college, they have had enough time and experience with other people to know things like their preferred study methods (solitary vs. group study), preferred rehearsal strategies (inward reflection vs. class discourse) and recreation styles (recharging by being alone vs. being with others).

Perhaps the most common motivational reason for students to study off campus is not the location, the religious freedom, or the monetary savings, but the belief that off-campus study will get you to your degree in the best way possible. This thought pushed me toward my goals. On the days when I wasn't inspired, I would look for motivation in the fact that my study was drawing me toward achieving my bachelor's degree. Sometimes just looking at the end goal would help. I would also remind myself of the reasons why I wanted to earn my degree. One of these was the opportunity to study a variety of topics at college level. Topics that had stood out during high school or that had been discussed by family and friends were now subjects I could study for college credit! History, math, scuba diving, orchestra, language, and psychology were largely motivating in and of themselves and presented quite a treat. For other subjects, such as science and personal finance (term vs. whole life insurance, anyone?), more extrinsic motivation was needed. Here was where it was important to step back and look at my overall goal of earning a degree. Usually, this comprehensive look at my goal would kick me back into gear.

WHAT MOTIVATES YOU?

To determine your own motivational factors, you will need to evaluate *why* you want to continue your education, and then, specifically, why you want to do so off campus. You won't need flowery, inspirationally-worded catch-phrases to keep the educational fire ablaze, but you will need at least one good reason for when the going gets tough. Take a moment to reflect:

- Am I studying off campus so my study can be more easily scheduled around my life and family?
- Are my studies improved when I am primarily responsible for creating my educational experience?
- Does the money I am saving encourage me to make the sacrifices needed to complete my degree?
- Is having the goal of earning a degree going to inspire me to finish?
- Am I proving to myself that I can conquer college?
- Is the knowledge I am internalizing keeping me energized?

If you can verbalize and even write down the select factors that inspire you to earn college credit, you will have a rationale to continue your education when it's not fun or easy.

If your reasons are less than positive ("My parents are making me," or "I don't have another choice for furthering my education," etc.), see if you can creatively reword those sentiments into uplifting action statements ("Because my parents are helping me fund my education, I am willing to give this method of learning a shot," or "I want to learn so badly that I will make this route work for me and my situation," etc.) Feeling trapped or forced into doing something is very demotivating for me, so I find it helpful to either reevaluate my decision or change my attitude rather than mask my disdain for my choices. I doubt I could have finished my degree if I felt someone or something was forcing me into college off campus.

This reminds me to mention that if you can throw out negative factors influencing your decision not to go on campus, you will have less stress and internal conflict. I say less because there will always be some stress and conflict, no matter how you complete college. People will be wary of your educational choices regardless of what those choices are. If you can have a maximum of inner peace while pursuing your goals, then you will be more resilient when the inevitable hurdles and naysayers appear.

To set yourself up for a productive and pleasant college experience, name your motivating factors. Find ways to exclude the negative aspects of your degree path, and remind yourself that you *do* have other options—options you have chosen to forgo in order to focus on this specific goal. Defining *why* you are earning a degree the way you are will keep purposefulness in your degree.

MOTIVATION AT THE MICRO LEVEL

What about motivation during a study of a single subject? Ah, this is a topic dear to my heart. For every subject with a credit-bearing test at the end, I followed a predictable pattern. My feelings about my learning took the same shape as a roller coaster track. Perhaps you can relate, even if you have never taken a credit-by-exam test.

1) Wow, a new subject to dive into! The information is foreign, stimulating, fresh, and provocative. At the same time, the basic aspects need to be internalized quickly as topics build upon one another, and if you don't watch out, you can wind up a third of the way through your study and find that there is "nothin' in my noggin'!" to quote Dory. Choosing resources can be a frustration, but a refresher of websites and publishers used for other subjects can help get the ball rolling.

2) After a few days (or maybe several hours, if you're a fast learner), you start to feel comfortable. The resources have gelled, and you know what to expect from your study time. You set some goals for yourself, including a possible test day.

3) It's been a week or two (or possibly less than a week for those fast learners whose study is highly condensed and concentrated), and now the boredom sets in. "I'm bored" was a phrase not allowed by my parents, so I say the word boredom with bated breath, and I say it only because it aptly describes how it feels to study for many days, in the same way, on the same topic. The newness and fun has worn off, the material is getting harder, memorization is now required, and studying has begun to feel routine. There are two ways to combat this study boredom, and the way you choose will depend on what you need. The first option is to introduce variety. This is an especially good option if you need to expand your knowledge. Add a supplemental text or try online flashcards. As for the second option, it is the opposite of the first. Sometimes when I felt the

need to broaden the range of information I was studying, what I really needed to do was forget variety and instead spend more time studying the resources I already had to hasten the testing day. This strategy helped me to dig deeper into my subject and add depth to my knowledge.

4) Now comes the awkward step: the pendulum swing between "Am I ready to take the test?" and "I am *so* ready to take the test!" I don't have many words of wisdom to offer here. This stage became easier as I took more tests, but I never skipped this stage. What's especially difficult about this phase is that it varies with the individual. My common refrain to "visit DegreeForum.net" won't definitively solve this stage. Still, DegreeForum.net users' comments did assist me many times in appraising my readiness to take a test; so at this point of test preparation, it *is* a good idea to visit DegreeForum.net. Completing this stage comes down to using practice tests to gauge your knowledge of the material, placating your nerves with "enough" study, and using your testing history to know how your practice test scores and emotions relate to your final test score.

5) The day of testing: please let me get it over with! The earlier in the day I could get into the testing room, the better. While in the testing room, not only was I racking my brain to find those tidbits of information, I was also in a duel with my emotions. Sentiments from all levels of self-confidence floated through my brain on nearly every exam. These ranged from "I've got this test—I might even ace it!" to "This question is taking forever to solve. I wonder how many more questions there are like this one. Perhaps I won't even get to all the questions!" to "I didn't know *this* would be on the test!"

6) The results:

  1) Pass—When I passed, I was thrilled! The perfectionist in me screamed in disappointment at my failure to earn a perfect score, but I was so glad to have that subject behind me that I soon warmed to my credit-earning score.

  2) Fail—As much I'd like to say I passed every exam I attempted, this would not be telling the truth, so let me showcase how it feels to fail: It hurts. It especially hurt when it was a subject I assumed would be simple, a thought that perhaps predicted my downfall. Two thoughts of relief even in

failure are: I wouldn't have to study that subject for a least a couple months (because of the mandatory retake waiting period), and the fact that I had learned some new information. Maybe the information wasn't enough to pass, but something I'd added to my mental arsenal could be (and has been) immensely valuable later in life.

3) Usually I was so happy to be done with that certain subject that beginning a new subject looked pretty tantalizing, even if it meant reliving the emotional roller coaster. I found it quite constructive to use the motivation gained in finishing one subject as impetus for launching my next subject.

PROCRASTINATION

A discussion of motivation would be incomplete without dealing with procrastination. I'd like to dismiss procrastination along with test failures, but that would be foolish. I have learned quite a bit about my ability to put things off just by admitting that I do, in fact, procrastinate. Foremost in this knowledge of procrastination is that *the decision to not make a decision is still a decision.* But how easy this is to forget!

Let's begin with the definition of procrastinate: *to put off or defer (an action) until a later time; delay. From Latin* prōcrāstināre *to postpone until tomorrow.*[66] From this definition, we might say that any action put aside temporarily has been subjected to procrastination. However, compare this with another definition of procrastination: *the act or habit of procrastinating, or putting off or delaying, especially something requiring immediate attention.*[67] Now we see that procrastination is an unresolved action that really should be addressed immediately and we are choosing to ignore it.

Also notice the word "habit" that has casually dropped into the second definition. The habit-forming aspect of procrastination probably cannot be overstated. "A little sleep, a little slumber, a little folding of the hands to rest, and poverty will come upon you like a robber, and want like an armed man."[68] It becomes terribly easy to find other fun and pressing activities when in avoidance mode. Even unpleasant tasks sound appealing. "Wow! Look at that pile of dishes! Wouldn't that be a nice thing to do for Mom? I'll just study later."

What are the results of procrastination? Putting things off unresolved can affect your options. Selecting study materials three days from your test date will afford you less flexibility in your resources than the same process three weeks prior to testing. The other downside to passively delaying decisions is you must think about them again. Instead of quietly fading into oblivion, they routinely crop up in your to-do list, weekend plans, and even daydreams!

During college, my procrastination hallmark was choosing to put off completing the most pressing activity (such as working my way through a textbook) and assuaging my conscience by tackling another, less odious activity (like looking for practice tests online). Although both activities needed doing, neglecting the most important task robbed me of any happiness I might have felt for completing at least one of the activities. Doing something for the sake of avoiding something else is depressing. (Nonetheless, this type of procrastination can be used to the student's advantage: find a task more unpleasant than study and procrastinate doing that task by studying! This technique is called structured or productive procrastination.[69])

Of course, procrastination can be quickly, though not effortlessly, remedied by starting and finishing the unpleasant task. One technique is to assign yourself a 20-minute period to work on the project you wish to avoid. The act of getting started will move you toward your goals and boost your morale. For the times you cannot start at the present moment, scheduling decisions and tasks will maximize time and mental effort, as waffling has been replaced with a specific time to start the assignment. So, while I am certainly at liberty to do dishes before I study, I should realize that I am choosing to postpone study. There is more freedom in purposeful choices than in waiting to be forced into an action or decision.

Procrastination can be beastly to uproot. To do this, we must find balance between putting off certain tasks because they aren't the highest priority and biting the bullet to get those tasks done. Achieving this balance is apparently a lifelong endeavor, as procrastination can sneak in at any time of life. The following section reveals a few techniques I currently employ to achieve my goals.

My Specific Study Habits

When I need to get some concentrated, productive study accomplished, these are some of the tools I put to use:
- Make a to-do list. I find that the process of sitting down to study

uncovers a nest of pressing loose ends and other unfinished projects. If I make a list of those activities, not only is my mind uncluttered, but I don't have to mentally rehearse my to-do list (consciously or subconsciously) while studying.

- Prioritize. Once I have created my to-do list, I can compare my activities for priority. If a family member is in the hospital, visiting them will outweigh study. However, checking up on my Etsy store can wait until after I study. I love this step because at the end of the day when I look at what I accomplished, having the highest-priority objectives accomplished makes me feel more confident than if I have ping-ponged from one activity to the next until bedtime.

- Put aside distractions. This sounds so uncomplicated...just set those disturbing people, events, and items out of the way. Can we all agree that this is far harder than it sounds? A few steps I take to make my job easier include:
    ° Physically moving to a quiet or semi-controlled area
    ° Giving my family and friends advance notice that I will be busy studying during a certain time of day or for a set number of hours
    ° Listening to instrumental music
    ° Capitalizing on the morning hours
    ° Checking for new texts/emails only on breaks

- Use a timer. I used to balk at the suggestion of this productivity aid, but I've recently found a timer to be quite motivating. Research regarding the use of study periods punctuated with short breaks shows focused performance and improved recall of the information presented.[70] A routine of 20-30 minutes followed by a 5-minute break with an additional 30-minute break after four study sessions is a common schedule known as the Pomodoro technique.[71] One of my favorite break activities is pushups.

- Work hard and then take a day off. God created us to work and then have a day of rest.[72] Both too much study and too little study are equally vicious, as each robs the learner of joy in life: in the first, the joy of rest after accomplishment, and in the other, the joy of hard work. I can attest to this from first-hand experience. I have been too busy and frenzied and have pushed myself to sickness, and I have been too lethargic and unmotivated and have missed goals.

- Vary your study resources. The relief gained by changing from 100% internet reading to 75% internet reading and 25% book reading can be amazing!
- Find a new study method. A simple internet search can expand your learning horizons. While too many new techniques at once can frustrate you and fragment your study, one new technique regularly added to your routine can build your incentive to hit the books.
- Change your location. I prefer to study at home, in a quiet room, but I do get tired of staring absently at the same wall or seeing the same knickknacks on either side of my laptop. Change it up—even a move of twelve feet can be enough. Others may enjoy taking their study to the library or coffee shop for a change in scenery.
- Build a reward system. In my senior year, I wasn't looking forward to my final eight DSST tests, especially the three days with two tests apiece. So I brainstormed a fun activity to do with my family after each test or set of tests. My schemes included visiting our new frozen yogurt shop, getting cupcakes, and going to Dairy Queen. You will probably want to augment these dessert-centric rewards with fun activities of your own.
- Pray. People who don't know me very well might think I'm perennially happy. Happiness is a big part of my personality. However, I didn't earn my degree with a strictly undaunted attitude and perpetual grin. There were tears, failures, let-downs, procrastination, and fear. When I'm at my wit's end, no amount of lists, timed sessions, and/ or study locations will solve my disarray. Even extra sleep, which clarifies many problems, won't solve everything. Here is when I turn to my Heavenly Father, who gives me refuge, protection, and purpose in life.[73] Only He can keep me from the ultimate futility of to-do lists and the potentially overwhelming disappointment of unfulfilled goals. Prayer is a tremendous help during periods of ennui.

WHEN THE GOING GETS TOUGH

During my third year in college and the beginning of the fourth, I had the feeling that college would go on forever! I live in a college town, with three institutions within a four-mile radius. I am surrounded by students, ex-students, and pre-students. Obviously the student lifestyle is quite prevalent.

Seeing, feeling, and participating in this college culture had me swimming in the middle of a college sea. On some days there was no land to be seen, and I felt like treading water was the best and most I could do. Those days were the ones where someone would hint that I wasn't really doing college or that I probably would never finish.

"Shake it off," I told myself. "I will only fail if I fail to try." My favorite motivational imagery is the duck letting water roll off his back. My mom has used this metaphor since I was little. Both she and my dad would remind me and my sister to take criticism, mistakes, and failure in stride, using it as motivation for growing, learning, and starting anew. It took many, many repetitions of this mental picture for me to fight my way through the sour days of college.

However, we all face doubters, critics, and challengers. These feelings of uncertainty and discomfort are universal, no matter what course of life is taken. Whether we tackle college or not, we will see opposition throughout our years. While I had anticipated others' skepticism, I had not expected my own temperament to include intermittent doubt about my set course. At times, I was my own worst enemy.

How are we to deal with these difficulties and emotions? Throughout the degree journey, practicing practical steps like reviewing personal reasons to get a degree, trying new study techniques, and quelling procrastination will not only enhance the outcome of the journey, but lay a foundation of habits to build upon throughout life. Certainly, a detachment between our feelings and our self-worth is crucial for surviving dubious seasons. A dependable support system should also be fostered, as discussed in the next chapter.

So, while in the midst of the college sea, most days I could see land and I swam strongly for it. After four long/short years, I did reach land. The era of study, roller coaster rides of test emotions, and college as top priority were, at least for a time, complete. As one of the best rewards from my experience, I was now accompanied by the habits and motivational tips that I had practiced for four years. Whatever projects I would take up next would have the benefit of being emboldened by what I learned and fought for in college.

TAKEAWAY TIPS

- Ask yourself, "Why am I earning this degree?" Your answers will help you advance through your journey.
- Identify what motivates you to learn, and create strategies to implement these motivating factors.
- Ride out the test emotions roller coaster. Taking tests does get easier with repetition.
- Kick procrastination to the curb.
- Remember you are never alone in any problem you face.

CHAPTER 8

WHERE TO GO FOR HELP?

Recently, I was talking to a cashier at my favorite local grocery store, Andy's Market. She asked me if I attended Walla Walla University just down the road. I replied that though I hadn't enrolled at WWU, I had taken CLEP tests there. "Have you heard of CLEP?" I asked.

She was aware of CLEP tests, but not familiar with them. I told her that CLEP tests were similar to testing out of a course and that they were different from online courses because of the self-paced schedule and the lack of a professor.

She thought about this and replied, "So where do you go when you need help?"

Considering the line of shoppers behind me, I gave a condensed response and said, "You can find resources online or reach out to someone in the community, like a local professor or a tutor."

However, these three are certainly not the only resources available for off-campus students. Students can get support from the college or university they plan to attend; this avenue of resources includes admissions counselors, advisors, and fellow students. Assistance can also come through textbooks, libraries, and mentors. If your family and friends are willing to collaborate, you can glean from their wisdom and encouragement. Community colleges are another resource. The type of support you choose will be based on your personal preferences, your community, and your enrollment status. Regardless of how much help you have through these groups, the most extensive and adaptable resource by far is the internet.

RESOURCES FOR THE OFF-CAMPUS STUDENT

The Internet

Of all the many study resources available, the internet stands out by offering the freedom to learn quietly and conveniently. Not only can you find information through a search engine or from colleges' websites directly, but you can also connect with others who have taken the off-campus journey and shared their findings along the way. The internet is home to a nearly unlimited number of paid and free resources. With this much information available, it often becomes challenging to wade through the numerous choices. So, how *do* you pinpoint what you need to know?

Sometimes answers are just a search engine away. Just type your question, such as "When is Thomas Edison State University's graduation?" directly into the search engine. If the results aren't helpful, reword your query. Employing another search provider can help as well.

You can also find information directly from the colleges of your choice. Typically the college's website will include a FAQ page, contact information, course listings and descriptions, pricing, and types of credit accepted (such as CLEP and DSST). While it seems obvious that this information would be included on the college's website, I am always amazed at how quickly I would forget to go to the website when I had questions.

During my degree journey, my favorite category of resources was information from other off-campus students. This knowledge from fellow learners was invaluable to me, as through it I could find answers to what turned out to be common problems. Questions that were answered through this method include: How do I begin to set up my degree plan? How difficult is DSST's History of the Soviet Union test? What are some pros and cons of each of the Big Three schools? Having a sounding board to hash out the day-to-day frustrations, the deal-breaker policies, and the overall goals of getting a degree was not only encouraging but valuable in terms of both time and money.

Using the internet can be enlightening, sobering, encouraging, and mystifying. Though it's often challenging to pinpoint the information you need, search engines, college websites, and personal testimonies will start you in the right direction, if not answer your questions. Don't hesitate to tap into this ever-expanding collection of information. Once you've found answers to your more basic and general questions, you are better equipped to visit with admissions counselors and advisors about your personal and individualized questions and problems.

Admissions Counselors

Even before you are ready to enroll to complete your degree, you can expect some help from the college you plan to attend. Admissions counselors are specifically tasked with assisting prospective students. This division of staff will help you transition from self-imposed structure and deadlines to those set by the college. They can also answer some of the issues related to your specific situation, such as inquiring about enrollment requirements, understanding tuition options, and estimating the transferability of the learning you currently possess (be it previously-earned college credits, certifications, military experience, etc.).

You may want to contact a college as a prospective student for a variety of reasons. I contacted admissions counselors at two schools to find out about getting credit for my CompTIA A+ computer certification because I needed more information than was listed on the colleges' websites. My sister requested information about tuition from the office of admissions prior to applying. Those returning to college will want to know if their credits from other schools or credit that is, say, 20 years old, will be accepted. Admissions counselors are your primary college contacts prior to enrollment, and they can help answer these types of questions.

Admissions counselors are a tremendous help during the transition of working toward your degree without college oversight to working directly with the college. After having your education and study customized to you *by* you, adjusting to the college's schedule may be frustrating—I certainly felt my share of frustration. Throughout the enrollment process, there are hoops to jump through, deadlines to meet, and questions that just aren't answered by reading the FAQs. Admissions counselors and the following category of college staff work together to provide critical support for the off-campus student.

Advisors

After the enrollment process is complete, new questions pop up regularly: What type of classes can be used in which degree? Where does my previously-earned college credit apply to my current degree? Who will tell me if my degree plan is accurate? What if I want to change my degree program? Where can I get advice and recommendations regarding these inquiries?

Enter advisors. Advisors fall into off-campus students' list of "Most Helpful People." The difference between advisors and admissions counselors is mainly in the enrollment status of the students they target. Whereas admissions counselors help prospective or matriculating students, advisors work solely with enrolled students. Advisors are prepared to help solve students' specific problems at the most personalized level. Typically, advisors specialize in one field of study, such as business or nursing. Often you can find advisors and their contact information listed on the college's website. At some colleges, you are assigned an advisor; at others, you get to choose your advisor. If you have the latter option, you might look for one who concentrates on your degree field or on non-traditional learning. See if you can infer from any of the advisors' biographies how well your plans and ambitions will match their specialties. Once you have either been matched with an advisor or you have selected one, the next step is to connect.

The process of reaching out to an advisor is straightforward, though there are several ways to go about it. Telephone and email are popular. I had great success using Thomas Edison State University's ticket system. (Currently you can launch a ticket directly from the university's website by signing in and visiting MyEdison.) The majority of the college websites I've visited over the years utilize a ticket or helpdesk system. While the ticket system is slightly more hassle than simply sending an email, creating a ticket allows the college to direct your inquiry to the appropriate staff member or department, thereby increasing the probability of expedient and pertinent service. The ticket system also has the advantage of being trackable.

Regardless of the method you choose, contacting your advisor gives you access to customized support and a mentor who is able to walk you through the nuances of credit earning. This exchange of information is not always easy. As in any conversation, patience and diligence are required to keep you and your advisor on the same page. However, the guidance and counsel found through an advisor are worth the time and effort required.

BRINGING YOUR GOALS TO LIFE

Something I learned from my advisor was the need to express aloud my underlying goals. Even though my advisor specialized in helping students use credit-by-exam tests to gain credit, he did not specifically steer me toward this method. This came as a surprise to me, as I had selected my advisor from a list of names with brief biographies and chosen him based on his credit-by-exam emphasis. Because it was his key field, I thought he would recommend this style of learning. This belief led to my mistake of not telling him that this was *my* preferred method. Evidently he assumed that I was interested in online courses, so he guided me in that direction.

This taught me a valuable point: If you want to earn credit by a specific method, tell your advisor. If you have specific time constraints, speak up! If saving money is critical to meeting your objectives, bring that up as well. Whatever your plan is, make sure you and your advisor are steering in the same direction. For the sake of both parties, it is advantageous that you speak plainly about what is most important in your situation: your time, your money, your preferred learning method, the type of degree you want to earn, the people you want to meet, and so on. The very core of an advisor's job is helping the student succeed, and he can do this more easily if he knows what he is helping you reach. The reverse is true as well. Your mentor has preferences and specialties, and he will lean toward those values, whether consciously or unconsciously. Be aware of this as you consider the advice given. With both sides' cards on the table, you can expediently use the advisor's counsel to alter your plans, continue your current heading, or perhaps chart a completely new course.

The reason it is so important to describe your goals to your advisor is because the definition of success varies from student to student. College-level learners have a multitude of goals and reasons for attending college, and there are just as many successful outcomes. Clearly outlining your goals is a terrific way to start many of the stages of distance learning, but it is especially important when you enroll or visit with an advisor. Don't worry if the only goal you can define is getting a degree. Take that as a foundation and add building blocks on top. What kind of degree are you pursuing? A bachelor's? A doctorate? Next you might ask what you hope to achieve once you have your degree. The clearer you make your goals, the easier it will be to explain them to your advisor, to your family and friends, and to other people you encounter. Remember that your goals can change as you move toward them, so it's good to have medium-sized goals, such as completing one year of college, alongside your large goals. Having goals of different lengths can be the most motivational way to go. While you take little bites of your elephant goal, you are being encouraged by the completion of your short-term goals.

Having a game plan is excellent, but don't let the lack of a plan stop you from asking for help. In this case, conversations with your advisor may include discussions of different strategies and options. I waited until I had most of my ducks in a row before contacting an advisor. This worked out alright, but I had deeply researched degree plans and strategies as well as gathered general tips for years from books, DegreeForum.net, and other websites. I did this because I usually prefer to find out as much information as possible on my own before approaching someone to ask for help.

However, had my inclinations been different, I would have needed to request help long before I enrolled my last year. While advisors can give you little, if any, help before you are an official student, there are other professionals, such as admissions counselors, who can help you before enrollment. I also recommend searching DegreeForum.net for learners who are taking similar classes or have a comparable learning background. If someone hasn't asked your question already (the search feature will help answer this), why not contact a user directly to ask how they did something, or better yet, start a thread with your question. At worst, your post may go unnoticed and you will have to try another avenue for help. At best, you will get several opinions and first-hand reports on how a strategy works and then you can add your own feedback as you go, enriching the online community and paying it forward.

How Will You Reach Your Goals?

While you are refining and clarifying your goals, you may want to take a look into the past at how you have been learning and where you go for advice. Noting these two aspects about yourself anytime during your degree journey (and especially once you enroll) can help you when the going gets tough. Here are some common learning styles I have noticed and their corresponding methods for getting advice:

LEARNER TYPE	POTENTIAL RESOURCES AND METHODS
"That's what friends are for" learner: Most successful with accountability partners; enjoys studying with others	• discussing ideas and options with family, mentors, and local professionals • admissions counselors/advisors • seeking out fellow off-campus students • signing up for a degree mentor through a third-party such as CollegePlus • using schedules created by mentor or advisor
"I get the best of both worlds" learner: Finds some things are more easily learned individually and other things are more easily learned in a group; enjoys self-directed study and guided study; may draw from a varying number of people for support	• online research • online forums • discussing ideas and options with family, mentors, friends, and local professionals • getting input from admissions counselors/advisors • seeking out fellow off-campus students • blending personally-set goals with recommended schedules from others

"I do it my way" learner: Likes to find things out for self; thrives on self-directed study; relies on small circle of family or friends for support	• online research • online forums • FAQ pages • discussing ideas and options with family and mentors • setting own goals and deadlines • emailing admissions counselors/advisors

Now, the learner types listed are certainly not as cut and dried as the chart would suggest. Using myself as an example, in my mathematics and history courses, I liked to find things out myself and organize a variety of methods to retain and recall the information I was learning. But for scuba diving, I enjoyed taking the course on campus rather than teaching myself. If you find you are struggling with a particular subject, consider trying different resources and methods to improve your performance.

BUILDING YOUR SUPPORT GROUP

No matter what your learning style is, there are inevitable times of challenge when you need outside help and encouragement. During these difficult spots, your support group can guide you. First, you need to have a support group. Creating, maintaining, and reaching out to your support group are critical parts of your degree journey. For the off-campus student, this support group includes admissions counselors, advisors and other college staff, as well as family, friends, and fellow college learners. By receiving advice and encouragement from your support group, you can surmount your current hurdle and move ahead to the next leg of your journey.

How do students create their personalized support group? Developing this group can be difficult because of the many options available, but you can narrow these options by noting what type of support is needed to resolve your questions. If you have a general question about off-campus learning, you might connect online with a fellow learner. If your question pertains directly to a certain college and its policy, try searching the college's website for information directly from the source. For more personalized questions about a certain college, contact an admissions counselor or advisor (depending on your enrollment status). If you are stumped while trying to learn new information, you may have luck finding an explanation online. Prefer to have new concepts explained in person? Tap into local teachers, tutors, or professionals. For the times you need encouragement, look to your family and close friends to help you find motivation to continue your journey.

Perhaps you like meeting weekly with fellow students and discussing the challenges of balancing school, work, and family. You may want to start a group in your area for students to meet and encourage one another. Maybe you are active in discussion forums and enjoy addressing your challenges there. Or perhaps your family is your favorite support system, and they are willing to be listening ears and brainstorming partners.

As you progress through your degree journey, proactively search out which forms of support are most helpful to your personal learning system. You may find that you gravitate toward a certain method or style. Because we are all slightly different in the way we learn and in the encouragement we find most motivating, identifying these helpful methods is a process of trial and error. Remind yourself to try a variety of assistance methods and not get frustrated or discouraged when one doesn't work out as well as you hoped. Good things can come from initial difficulty, just as they did when I first phoned my advisor. Sometimes patience with a certain method will bear fruit. On the flip side, if there is no reason to hope for fruit, do stick your neck out and explore other avenues for assistance. Kindness, persistence, and the golden rule will take you far when searching for help and support.

During college, the support you require will change as your preferences and circumstances change. Don't be afraid to try something different if your current learning style isn't working. Ask others what their favorite methods are. While working on this book, one of my friends reminded me how motivating it is to get work done in the morning without procrastinating. I began writing in the morning, and almost immediately I saw my mood and work output improve. Little tips like these can help buffer you from the difficult or frustrating aspects of the college journey and make the journey itself equally as meaningful as the destination. Surround yourself with a support environment, nurture those relationships, and press on toward your goals!

TAKEAWAY TIPS

- Use the internet, admissions counselors, and advisors to guide your journey.

- When your efforts of searching for support seem to fizzle, look at the big picture. Is this a new strategy? Let it have some time to grow. Is this method just not working even after some time? Try something different.
- Flesh out your goals and share them with your advisors and others in your support system.
- Create and sustain a support system by reaching out to family, faculty, and other students.

CHAPTER 9

ACCREDITATION

When I began to research which college to attend, I hadn't chosen a major nor settled on specific post-college goals. There were two things I knew: I wasn't planning to pursue a medical or law degree, and I was intrigued by several degree majors (mathematics, music, history, and jewelry design). Even though I wasn't sure which degree I would choose, I wanted to be sure that my degree would be accepted by future employers and colleges/universities offering graduate education.

It was during my research of various degrees that I first learned about accreditation: recognition by a certain organization that a college or university meets the requirements set by the organization. However, some of this research was frustrating because I didn't know how U.S. colleges were regulated nor where to look for information about accreditation. Not being familiar with the structure of accreditation made it difficult to determine the legitimacy of a degree that could be completed entirely off campus.

Now that I have finished my degree, knowledge about college accreditation is just as important as when I was selecting and working toward my degree. Not only do I want to know that an employer or another school would respect my degree, I want to know *why* my degree is respected. As it turns out, having this information in my memory isn't useless now that I've chosen my school and graduated. It comes in very handy when I tell others about off-campus learning and how I achieved my degree. This information is also helpful when interviewing for a job: say your potential employer looks farther than just the name of your degree and alma mater and wants to know more about your degree—why you earned it and how. Here is where you can share your rationale for earning your degree off campus, creating your own support system, and choosing your college.

In this chapter, I will showcase the accreditation structure for U.S. higher education. While not complicated, accreditation does contain its own nuances like any other regulating framework. Being acquainted with these nuances is critical when choosing a college and a degree that will be an asset to your life. Plus, taking time to understand the regulation of colleges gives you grounded confidence in the off-campus method and reveals differences between scam and legitimate colleges.

COLLEGE ACCREDITATION IN THE UNITED STATES

To research college education earned on or off campus, it is important to have standards by which you can measure each school. These standards allow you to compare colleges with the assurance that a degree obtained off campus will be given the same recognition by other schools and employers as a traditionally-earned degree. Standards also assist you in deciding if the learning you receive off campus is the same quality as that earned on campus. Accreditation is a key standard that students, employers, and educational institutions themselves use to efficiently appraise higher education.

For institutions of higher education in the United States, accreditation itself is voluntary and nongovernmental. Though the government does not accredit *schools*, it does play a role in the accreditation structure. That role is to help its citizens determine the effectiveness of accrediting *agencies*: how accurately these agencies monitor institutions' quality. The government became involved after World War II, when the GI Bill (Servicemen's Readjustment Act of 1944) prompted government oversight of accreditation. The Veteran's Readjustment Assistance Act of 1952 called for the secretary of education to put forth a list of accrediting agencies.[74] The listed agencies are included based on meeting certain criteria, including having experience in accrediting institutions, using evaluation standards, ensuring that these standards are met, and other qualifying factors.

Who Are the Accrediting Bodies?

There are several levels of accreditation. Here is a pictorial overview:

ACCREDITATION

United States Department of Education (ED) / Council for Higher Education Accreditation (CHEA)

Regional Accreditors (6)

National Accreditors (50+)

- Higher Learning Commission
- Middle States Commission on Higher Education
- New England Association of Schools and Colleges
- Northwest Commission on Colleges and Universities
- Southern Association of Colleges and Schools
- Western Association of Schools and Colleges

Three examples of the many national accreditors:
- American Occupational Therapy Association Accreditation Council for Occupational Therapy Education
- Association for Biblical Higher Education Commission on Accreditation
- Distance Education Accrediting Commission

At the top level are two organizations that can be thought of as clearinghouses. Their purpose is to regulate the accrediting agencies or, to put it another way, accredit the accreditors.

1) The United States Department of Education (ED) provides a list of accrediting agencies that meet the criteria set by the head of the ED, the secretary of education. The ED does not accredit educational institutions and/or programs.[75]
2) The Council for Higher Education Accreditation (CHEA), an organization governed by a 20-person board composed of college/university presidents, institutional representatives and members of the public, recognizes accrediting agencies that are regional, faith-related, career-related, and programmatic.[76]

As of March 2016:

- 52 accreditors were recognized by ED,
- 61 accreditors were recognized by CHEA, and
- 27 of these accreditors were both ED- and CHEA-recognized.[77]

Below ED and CHEA is a secondary level of accreditors who directly certify colleges and universities. These accreditors fall into one of two categories: regional or national.

Regional Accreditation

Regional accreditation is available for public, private nonprofit, and private for-profit colleges/universities that not only meet a rigorous set of standards, but are also located within one of six regions of the United States, such as New England. There are five agencies recognized by both ED and CHEA and one that is only recognized by the ED:

1) Higher Learning Commission (formerly North Central Association of Colleges and Schools)
2) Middle States Commission on Higher Education
3) New England Association of Schools and Colleges, Commission on Institutions of Higher Education
4) Northwest Commission on Colleges and Universities (The commission's CHEA recognition expired in 2012 and has not been renewed by the commission.)
5) Southern Association of Colleges and Schools
6) Western Association of Schools and Colleges (This association has three components, two of which relate to colleges: the Accrediting Commission for Community and Junior Colleges and the WASC Senior College and University Commission.)

Regional accreditation is not given to a single program or course; rather, the entire institution is given accreditation. To be regionally accredited, an institution must undergo a period of mandatory observation and review. A few of the many standards that are assessed before accreditation is given include the school's policies, faculty, infrastructure, mission statement, and the school's ability to meet its educational objectives in upcoming years. Regional accreditation is "an ongoing status that must be reaffirmed periodically."[78]

National Accreditation

National accreditors endorse trade and vocational schools, colleges, and universities offering degrees that are focused on a specific job or skill. Over 50 national accrediting agencies exist. Three examples are the American Occupational Therapy Association Accreditation Council for Occupational Therapy Education, the Association for Biblical Higher Education Commission on Accreditation, and the Distance Education Accrediting Commission. To earn national accreditation, a college or school completes the application process set by the accreditor, including a review of the school conducted by the accrediting agency. Once accreditation is earned, it must be renewed periodically, and the school or program is monitored for continued compliance to the agency's guidelines.

National accreditation can be institutional, meaning the entire institution is accredited, or it can be programmatic, where only a specific program within the institution is accredited. For example, podiatric programs and schools can be accredited by the American Podiatric Medical Association Council on Podiatric Medical Education; Christian master's degree and doctorate programs can be accredited by the Association of Theological Schools in the United States and Canada Commission on Accrediting; and institutions offering degree programs designed to educate students for professional, technical, or occupational careers can be accredited by the Accrediting Council for Independent Colleges and Schools. Degrees that have national accreditation may not fit into a "traditional" degree model, often due to the specificity of the degree material.

Regional versus National Accreditation

Regional accreditors have become known for having more stringent qualification requirements than their national counterparts, though this is not always the case. Actually, regional and national accreditation share many aspects of their accreditation standards, and some schools that are regionally accredited will also obtain national accreditation for certain degree programs. Despite these similarities, regional accreditation is viewed by most colleges as more prestigious than national accreditation.

The main reason for this distinction is due to the type of programs covered by regional and national accreditation. Regionally accredited schools typically offer standardized degrees that fall into conventional college education categories, and their accreditation covers all the degrees offered by the school. Nationally accredited schools focus more on certificates, licenses, and vocational degrees or certifications, and their accreditation can cover a single degree offered by the school or all the degrees offered.

Because degrees from schools that are not trade or vocational have more in common, allowing for easier comparison, and because of the current bureaucratic structure, credits from a school with regional accreditation transfer far more widely and easily than credits from a school with solely national accreditation. Credit earned at a nationally accredited school does not transfer well to a regionally accredited school. It may not transfer at all. This has a large effect on higher education and transferring college credit. Professions that typically require earning your education at a regionally accredited school include nursing, pharmacy, psychology, and teaching. Courses taken at nationally accredited schools will rarely count toward earning the licenses needed to practice in these fields.

This is not to say that national accreditation is meaningless. There are fields where earning a degree with national accreditation can get you working in your profession without needing to attend a regionally accredited school. In fields such as medicine, engineering, and veterinary medicine, regional accreditation may not be required, but specific national accreditation will. For example, the national accreditation usually required for the three fields just listed is:

- Liaison Committee on Medical Education or American Osteopathic Association for physicians
- ABET (Accreditation Board for Engineering and Technology) for engineers
- American Veterinary Medical Association's Council on Education or Committee on Veterinary Technician Education and Activities for veterinarians

If you know you will be pursuing one of these fields or a related field, regional accreditation or specific national accreditation will be a primary factor in your comparison of schools and programs.

Besides preparing you for a specific career field, choosing an appropriately accredited degree will equip you to continue your education. In her book, *Homeschooling for College Credit*, Jennifer Cook-DeRosa explains that nationally accredited credit may not transfer to a regionally accredited school, and, drawing on her own experience, she emphasizes that earning credit that only carries national accreditation may force you to begin your degree from scratch should you wish to go back to school. When considering a professional, vocational, or trade-related degree or program, Cook-DeRosa suggests you take a look at your options. Instead of a nationally accredited trade school, you may be able to attend a regionally accredited community college to earn not only equal education, but also credits you can use later in life.[79]

How Do I Find the Accreditation of a Particular School?

To view the accreditation of a potential school, you can visit the college's website directly, or use the U.S. Department of Education's Office of Postsecondary Education's Database of Accredited Postsecondary Institutions and Programs.[80] You can also visit another third-party website that offers accreditation information about colleges.

Policies for accepting credit from nationally accredited schools are not always laid out clearly by regionally accredited colleges.[81] This makes it difficult for students to know if their credits will transfer between colleges without contacting the individual schools and presenting their scenario. Transferring credit occurs frequently in off-campus learning, so it can be essential to the success of your degree to know in advance how the credits you have earned or plan to earn will transfer.

Earning credits from a regionally accredited college greatly boosts the credits' transferability. This is one reason why you want to see that your college/university is accredited by the appropriate regional accrediting agency (i.e., Southern Association of Colleges and Schools Commission on Colleges) when selecting a college.

If you are considering earning credits from a nationally accredited school and you plan to transfer these credits to another school, it is very important to check with the school to which you plan to transfer the credits and verify that your credits will be accepted.

If you have already earned credits from a nationally accredited school and you wish to transfer them, contact the school receiving the credit to learn about their credit acceptance policy. Sometimes this policy is available on the school's website.

THE JOB OF ACCREDITATION

Accreditation is a valuable subject to research. It provides a starting point for comparing colleges. It comes into play not only when transferring credits, but when applying for a job and continuing your education. And, it's useful in casual conversation when discussing the validity of a degree earned off campus.

There are two things to remember about accreditation which will help you earn long-lasting and portable credits:[82]

1) Credit from regionally accredited colleges has a far better chance of successfully transferring to another school.
2) Regionally accredited schools carry more clout than nationally accredited schools.

Armed with knowledge about the structure of accreditation, students comparing schools can shift their focus from uncertainty about a school's legitimacy and instead discover which school offers programs and features most beneficial to them.

TAKEAWAY TIPS

- The United States Department of Education (ED) and the Council for Higher Education Accreditation (CHEA) accredit the accreditors. They comprise the top level of accreditation.
- Regional and national accreditation form the next layer. Regional accreditation has more clout.
- Credit from regionally accredited schools transfers more easily than credit from nationally accredited schools.
- You can find the accreditation of a particular school by going to the school's website or by visiting the government's accreditation database: http://ope.ed.gov/accreditation/.

CHAPTER 10

CHOOSING YOUR DEGREE, FINDING YOUR SCHOOL

To move forward with my goal of trying off-campus learning for one year, I needed to select both a major and a college. I began to brainstorm. I started a notebook where I could compile my thoughts and questions about college. At the beginning of the notebook, I listed my college goals and degree interests. These degree interests ranged from photography to food preparation to natural sciences/mathematics.

I didn't come to a decision about my major quickly. I looked at my varied interests, most of which seemed exciting and appealing, and I thought how lucky I would be to study some of these subjects *for school*. However, practicality soon set in, and I knew that besides enjoying what I was studying, it was also important to have a degree that I could see using in the near future—a degree that would bring me closer to my life's aspirations.

Because almost all of the majors I was considering could make use of credit-by-exam tests, I decided to get started studying and taking tests before I finalized my degree choice. I began my college freshman year by studying for a few general CLEP exams as I deliberated on my choice of a major for about a month. The post-college goals I had in mind (starting my own business and homeschooling my children, if children were in my future) didn't require a specific degree. So, rather than search for a particular degree major, I instead focused on finding a degree where what I learned would benefit these goals.

Since the type of information I would be learning was more important than the major listed on my diploma, I needed to choose a major that would allow me to reach my current goals: complete college for a reasonable fee and pursue a degree while exploring different practical topics to improve my education and well-roundedness as an individual. A natural sciences/ mathematics major seemed to fulfill these goals.

This month of deliberation was not the last time I analyzed my choice of a major. I revisited this decision at the beginning of my college senior year. Even at that point, it took me nearly a month yet again to mentally finalize which major would best serve me. The importance of my degree's long-term use made me take my time before reaching a decision.

What I learned through the experience of selecting a major was empathy for other students who don't know which major to choose. Higher education has two contrasting goals: on one hand, students are expected to stretch their educational boundaries and grow by learning completely new information, regardless of its practicality. On the other hand, students understand that future job opportunities and success come from careful preparation applicable toward the employment field they plan to enter. Balancing these two objectives can make choosing a degree major difficult.

For other students, they know just what degree they need to reach their next goals in life, and this makes the process of choosing a degree more straightforward. Once a student knows which degree he wants, he can focus on selecting a college.

What Degree Should Students Choose if They Have Identified Their Future Career?

Congratulations for knowing which profession you want to pursue! Having this heading for your degree journey will help you tremendously, even if you change your mind as you go along.

First, look at your profession. What certifications are required? What will your résumé need to look like for you to get your dream job? These questions will help you determine the degree major you will pursue and what level of education you will need.

After you assess your answers, you will have created parameters to use as you search for the appropriate degree. Here are some things to keep in mind when searching for this degree:

- Your degree should be something that directly moves you toward your life's goals.
- Your degree should be personally enriching. Yes, there will probably be a few courses that you aren't thrilled to take, but overall, your degree should be something that makes you excited to study and learn.

What Degree Should Students Choose if They Haven't Identified Their Future Career?

If you don't know which profession you will be pursuing, choosing your degree can be more difficult. Nevertheless, you can use many of the same principles as above. Think about how getting a degree will help your life goals. Earning a bachelor's degree helped me reach my goals of continuing my education after high school and exploring various topics at the college level.

You may find it useful to read What Color Is Your Parachute? *for advice on job and career choices.*

What Degree Should Adults Choose if They Are Returning to School to Further Their Career?

First, inventory your strengths. Then decide if a degree using those strengths moves you toward your life goals. Next, search for a college with an applicable program, perhaps even one that specializes in your career area. For example, if you are a police officer, you may look for a college that has a specific program for police officers who wish to "cash in" their work experience, fulfill the remaining credit requirements, and earn a degree.

CHOOSING A COLLEGE

Former Harvard President Derek Bok writes in his book, *Universities in the Marketplace*, "No reliable method yet exists that allows students to determine where they will learn the most."[83] Jeffrey Selingo echoes this position in his book *College (Un)Bound* when he writes, "As much as we spend on higher education, no bottom-line evaluation method exists for measuring what actually happens in the classroom and how that eventually translates into the value of the degree."[84] While these statements may seem blatantly obvious, they do succinctly explain why students today face confusion in choosing a college.

Selecting the right college is one of the most important choices in the college journey. The college you choose does have an effect on your learning and the outcome of your degree journey. This is because the one or more colleges that are part of your degree journey are your partners. In a partnership, the ideals, goals, and motivations of both parties bear on the outcome of the partnership. In the case of students and colleges, things that the college stands for change the college experience for the student. If the college promotes off-campus learning, you will be more likely to find assistance and understanding when completing a degree this way.

Finding a college tailored to you can be made easier by learning from others who have gained credit for similar experiences. You can locate people with similar goals on DegreeForum.net and through search engines. I've found that the time spent choosing a college with strengths that are advantageous to you pays dividends throughout the process of getting your degree.

In *College (Un)Bound*, Jeffrey Selingo has crafted questions for potential students and their parents to ask about a college before the student applies. This checklist is spread over topics such as return on the student's tuition investment, mobility of credits, course rigor, job preparation, and financial practices of the college. I highly recommend these questions, which are compiled near the end of the book in a section entitled "Checklist for the Future."

For information regarding the graduation rates of many two- and four-year colleges and universities, both public and private, visit http://collegecompletion. chronicle.com/. *Beyond the percentage of students who exit a particular college with a degree, the website also shows the average cost of tuition and student debt at individual institutions across the nation.*

How Did I Choose Thomas Edison State University?

Some students know which degree they will be pursuing before they know which school they will attend. Others are just the opposite. I was one of the latter students—I selected a college first, then a specific degree. I chose Thomas Edison State University (TESU) mainly because I could earn my degree using the non-traditional methods I was interested in trying and because many of their degrees fit my price range. However, I sorted through many colleges before I decided on TESU. I considered attending a community college, a women's college, and a Christian college before I ever thought to attend one of the Big Three. How did I narrow it down to Thomas Edison?

My decision was definitely influenced by *Accelerated Distance Learning*. A graduate of Thomas Edison State University himself, author Brad Voeller included many first-person descriptions of what it was like to earn a degree there. He also featured other alumni and students earning a degree from TESU. From these examples I could see TESU would be a good match for me.

I also considered Charter Oak State College and Excelsior College since they had many similarities to Thomas Edison. Being able to earn a degree completely through distance learning techniques from any of these three was important, especially since all three are located on the opposite side of the country from my home.

I also liked their open credit acceptance policies. Currently, the three schools will apply between 114 to 119 credit-by-exam tests and/or prior learning credits toward the total 120 credits needed for a bachelor's degree, meaning a student may only need to take one class from the school itself to graduate.

In the end, my choice of Thomas Edison State University boiled down to a good match between the following three components: my budget, TESU's areas of concentration (specifically, the natural science/mathematics concentration), and TESU's generous credit-by-exam acceptance policy.

The Cost Variable

In the spirit of remembering that colleges are businesses, Derek Bok notes there is the potential for colleges to create online classes solely for profit. He cautions that classes like these may not use technology to its full potential (because to do so would minimize profit), and may have had other corners cut that reduce quality.[85] While competition among colleges and the proliferation of online courses available has mitigated the amount of exploitation in online courses, it is crucial to keep in mind what you are receiving for your money when considering any type of college course.

In *Higher Education in the Digital Age*, William G. Bowen makes an excellent point about the cost of earning a degree. Even though we tend to focus on the cost per credit or the cost of college per year, another way to measure the cost of college is the "cost per degree conferred."[86] Calculating the total cost to achieve a certain degree can help give a long-term perspective to a prospective degree. Cost per degree encourages questions such as, "If I spend this money, how long before I recoup this cost through employment?" or "Is the knowledge I will gain on this journey worth its price tag?" Certainly, as Bowen notes, the cost per degree conferred is not a flawless measure of a degree (because there is worth in learning that doesn't result in a degree and because not all degrees are "created equal"). However, measuring a degree in this way prompts questions that are helpful in choosing a degree and comparing available options.

Cost and the Undecided Major

Earning a degree using distance learning methods can be a terrific use of time and money for many students for a variety of reasons, but especially if you haven't yet decided on a major. Why? Distance learning allows you to move forward toward a degree while discovering what you want to study. This off-campus scenario is similar to attending college on campus as a freshman with an undeclared major except in one important regard: cost.

Using the example of credit-by-exam tests, suppose you decide to test out of your first year of college classes using CLEP tests. You take 5-10 tests your first year and walk away with 30 credits. Then, you decide to radically change course in your college journey—say you are considering enrolling at a school that doesn't accept CLEP tests. Now what?

You have at least three options. You might postpone enrollment, continue testing for another year, transfer your credits to a college that does accept CLEP, and earn your associate degree. You could then transfer your associate degree to the school that doesn't accept CLEP tests. Another alternative would be to explore other schools that do accept CLEP tests. Or, in an unlikely scenario, you might decide to start over. The latter case is the only one where your money spent on CLEP tests benefited only your knowledge-related goals, instead of both knowledge- and degree-related goals.

How much would this year of credit-by-exam tests cost? Taking 5-10 CLEP tests requires between $550 and $1,100 (plus approximately $400-$600 for the cost of study materials).[87] This isn't chump change, but compare the high-end yearly figure, $1,100, with the average cost of attending college, say a public school as an in-state student, for one year: $9,410 (not including the cost of books and supplies, which hovers around $1,200 annually).[88]

If you took your freshman year of classes on campus and then changed your mind about what you wanted to study and had to begin again, you would have spent $9,139 plus textbook expenses, whereas if you spent the year taking CLEP tests and then changed your mind, you would have spent $1,100 plus money for study materials. Taking credit-by-exam tests not only saves you eight *thousand* dollars in one year alone, but it also limits your freshman year expenses should you choose to change course educationally and start over.

The first year of college is the ideal time to use credit-by-exam tests, especially for students with undeclared majors. Of all the four years of college, the coursework in the first year is the easiest to learn, access, and transfer due to its foundational level. Like any strategy, there are always exceptions, such as when a student decides to study on campus to be eligible for interning at the college at the same time. However, for many students, and especially those with undeclared majors, off-campus learning is efficient and less costly.

The power of credit-by-exam testing is perfectly illustrated in the freshman year. Having this flexibility and affordability available for even one-quarter of your bachelor's degree can dramatically affect your college experience. Because of the low risk associated with credit-by-exam testing, it's worth taking the time to research colleges that offer degrees that can be completed, at least in part, using distance learning methods. In the next section, I will highlight the Big Three colleges, which specialize in non-traditional education and have tailored their policies to support off-campus students.

BENEFITS OF THE BIG THREE

The Big Three colleges cater to the adult learner who may not be able to attend college on campus and to the motivated high school or college-age learner who has put a priority on self-directed learning. All three colleges accept CLEP and DSST tests, have a generous community college credit acceptance policy, are regionally accredited, and offer a variety of degree majors or concentrations that can be completed off campus if desired. For reference, I have compiled a synopsis of Big Three facts. If you are interested in more details of why these three colleges are known as the Big Three and how each is unique from the others, discussions of these topics can be found on DegreeForum.net.

Charter Oak State College

Located in New Britain, Connecticut, this school is regionally accredited through the New England Association of Schools and Colleges. Formed in 1973, the college's vision statement is "Charter Oak State College: A dynamic community of online learners advancing the nation's workforce one graduate at a time." To be admitted, the college requires students to be 16 years or older and possess nine or more acceptable college-level credits (these credits could be earned through credit-by-exam tests, and this requirement will be a non-issue if you postpone enrollment while earning credit as discussed in chapter 3).[89]

To graduate, you will need to complete a three-credit cornerstone course and a three-credit capstone course in your concentration.[90] There is a limit of 87 credits that can be transferred from community colleges.[91]

Tuition for online courses is calculated per credit; 2016-2017 rates are $287 for Connecticut residents and $377 for non-residents.[92] Degrees are conferred three times yearly, and there is an annual graduation ceremony.

Excelsior College

"What you know is more important than where or how you learned it®" is the philosophy of Excelsior College. The college was founded in Albany, New York, in 1971 and is regionally accredited by the Middle States Commission on Higher Education. There is no age requirement for admission; students who have not earned their high school diploma are eligible for admission with some stipulations.[93]

A three-credit capstone course (offered online) must be taken to graduate from Excelsior. All undergraduate degrees also require completion of a three-credit information literacy course, though it does not need to be earned from Excelsior.[94] The college's policy on community college credit is to accept 105 credits.[95]

For undergraduate students, the per-credit tuition rate is $510 for the 2016-2017 school year.[96] Graduation conferrals occur monthly with an annual commencement ceremony.

Thomas Edison State University

Thomas Edison State University of Trenton, New Jersey, was established in 1972 and is regionally accredited by the Middle States Commission on Higher Education. The university's mission statement is "Thomas Edison State University provides flexible, high-quality, collegiate learning opportunities for self-directed adults." To apply, students must be 21 or older and possess a high school diploma or GED. Students who do not meet these requirements may request special consideration and be accepted on a case-by-case basis.[97] (My sister and I were both accepted while under 21, and we had no trouble with the application process. Applicants under 21 are required to send their high school transcript and write a letter about themselves stating why they would be a good candidate.)

All bachelor's degree programs require a one-credit cornerstone course, and bachelor's degree programs with the notable exception of the Bachelor of Science in Business Administration require a three-credit capstone course to be taken from the university. TESU accepts 80 community college credits and 120 from a regionally accredited four-year institution.[98]

For online courses, the per-credit cost varies depending on which of the three tuition plans you choose: tuition per credit for the Comprehensive Tuition Plan and Per Credit Tuition Plan varies between $176-$385 for New Jersey residents and $260-$499 for out-of-state residents for the 2016-2017 school year.[99] Students can graduate at one of the four times per year and attend the annual commencement ceremony.

What Are Some Main Differences between These Schools?

Currently, policies at the Big Three schools are quite aligned. However, each school offers degrees in its own manner, according to its own policies. Thus, you may find that one of the three schools provides the particular degree you need or that one school maintains bachelor's degree requirements that make it easier to continue to graduate work. For degrees requiring specific programmatic accreditation in addition to regional accreditation, such as nursing or engineering degrees, you may find a better fit at one college depending on the degrees available and their programmatic accreditation.

The differences between the three colleges become clearer when you have selected the degree and major you wish to pursue. Once you have this information, you can compare the degree course outlines from each of the three colleges, as well as any course outlines from other colleges you are considering.

Comparing Bachelor of Science Degrees from the Big Three

Let's take the example of a Bachelor of Science in Business.
- First, we locate the page for the Bachelor of Science in Business on each college's website (the endnotes that follow include a direct link for each degree plan). Right away, we notice a few differences: the three schools use slightly different naming structures for their business degrees; these are shown in the table below.

SCHOOL	CHARTER OAK STATE COLLEGE	EXCELSIOR COLLEGE	THOMAS EDISON STATE UNIVERSITY
BACHELOR'S DEGREE TYPE:	Bachelor of Science	Bachelor of Science in Business	Bachelor of Science in Business Administration
CONCENTRATION/ MAJOR:	• Business Administration	• Accounting • Finance • General Business • Global Business • Management of Human Resources • Management Information Systems • Marketing • Operations Management	• Accounting • Accounting/CPA • Computer Information Systems • Entrepreneurship • Finance • General Management • Hospital Healthcare Administration • Human Resources/Organizational Management • International Business • Marketing • Operations Management

As we familiarize ourselves with each plan, we notice that Thomas Edison offers 11 areas of study within the Bachelor of Science in Business Administration program. These majors range from entrepreneurship to hospital healthcare administration. Any of these concentrations will still result in a diploma that reads Bachelor of Science in Business Administration, but the concentration portion of each degree plan is slightly different.

To analyze the Bachelor of Science in Business from each of the Big Three, we begin by looking at the business concentrations in a comparable business major across the three schools. I will use marketing as our example major, except for the major from Charter Oak State College, which strictly offers a Business Administration major.

Charter Oak State College:

Bachelor of Science in Business Administration: 120 credits, including 60 liberal arts, satisfaction of general education requirements, and a concentration of 45 credits.[100]

CONCENTRATION REQUIREMENTS:

Business Administration Major Requirements:		27 credits
ACC 101 Financial Accounting	MKT 220 Principles of Marketing	
ACC 102 Managerial Accounting	FIN 210 Financial Management	
BUS 120 Business Law	MGT 315 Organizational Behavior	
MGT 101 Principles of Management	MGT 499 Strategic Management Capstone	
ITE 101 Management Information Systems		

Business Administration majors must complete 9 upper level credits in one of the concentrations below:

- Small Business
- Project Management
- Human Resources
- Organizational Management
- General Business (developed with Academic Advisor)

Prerequisites:	9 credits

- Macroeconomics
- Microeconomics
- Business Statistics

Excelsior College:

Bachelor of Science in Business (Marketing): 120 credits, including the 60-credit arts and sciences component, the 54-credit business component, and the 6-credit additional credit component.[101]

BUSINESS COMPONENT REQUIREMENTS:

BUSINESS COMPONENT				Credit Hours
Business Core Requirements	Credit Hours		Credit Hours	
Financial Accounting	3	Principles of Management	3	
Managerial Accounting	3	Principles of Marketing	3	
Introduction to Business Law (United States Business Law)	3	Financial Management	3	33
Business Communication	3	International Business	3	
Computers	3	BUS 499 Strategic Management (capstone)①	6	
Business Electives				6
Concentration requirements *Must complete 15 credits in the concentration area of which 9 credits must be upper-level.*				15
Upper-Level Business Requirements *Must complete a minimum of 21 credits at the upper level of which 9 credits must be in the concentration.*				
MINIMUM BUSINESS COMPONENT				**54**

① **BUS 499 Strategic Management** is the required capstone course and must be taken through Excelsior College and cannot be transferred in.

Thomas Edison State University:

Bachelor of Science in Business Administration degree in Marketing: 120 credits, including 60 general education requirements, 36 professional business requirements, 18 "Area of Study: Marketing" credits, and 6 free electives.[102]

CONCENTRATION REQUIREMENTS	54
A. Professional Business Requirements	36
• Financial Accounting	(3)
• Managerial Accounting	(3)
• Business Law	(3)
• Principles of Management	(3)
• Computer Concepts and Applications/Introduction to Computers/CIS	(3)
• Introduction to Marketing	(3)

• Principles of Finance	(3)
• Business in Society or International Management	(3)
• Macroeconomics	(3)
• Microeconomics	(3)
• Business/Managerial Communications	(3)
• Strategic Management	(3)
B. Area of Study: Marketing	18
• Required Subjects	
• Marketing Research	(3)
• Electives	(15)
• Advertising	
• Advanced Advertising	
• Advanced Marketing Research	
• Advertising Campaigns	
• Advertising Copy and/or Layout	
• Advertising Media	
• Applied Marketing	
• Channels of Distribution	
• Creating & Implementing the Electronic Enterprise	
• Direct Mail and Direct Response Advertising	
• Direct Marketing Management	
• Franchising Management	
• Industrial Marketing or Business-to-Business Marketing	
• International Advertising	
• International Marketing	
• Introduction to Retailing Management	
• Leading Teams and Groups or Work Groups in Organizations	
• Legal Problems of the Marketing Process	
• Marketing Communications	
• Marketing Management	
• Marketing Management Strategy	
• Mathematical Models of Marketing Analysis	
• Marketing with Electronic Media	
• Merchandising	
• New Product Development & Marketing	

• Principles of Sales	
• Product Planning and Development	
• Public Relations: Thought and Practice	
• Research Methods in Organizations	
• Retail Advertising	
• Retail Buying or Sales Promotion or Visual Merchandising	
• Retail Buying and Merchandise Management	
• Retail Management	
• Sales Management	
• Services Marketing	
• Small Business Management	
• Supply Chain Management	

We can now go through and compare individual courses in each plan. Things I notice are:

- As noted earlier, the Bachelor in Science of Business Administration from Thomas Edison State University does not require you to complete a capstone course through TESU to graduate. (A one-credit cornerstone course is required.)
- All three degrees are comprised of 120 credits.
- Charter Oak allows for 6 business elective credits within the concentration, Excelsior allows 0, and Thomas Edison allows 15.
- Each degree concentration contains the following courses: Financial Accounting, Managerial Accounting, Business Law, Principles of Management, and Strategic Management.

Next, review your undergraduate and post-graduate goals for any nitty-gritty requisites that your bachelor's degree should have to make those goals possible. For this Bachelor of Science in Business example, I went to the websites of three schools offering graduate degrees to view the requirements for admission into their graduate school of business. This step allows me to prepare for graduate school while earning my bachelor's degree.

- At Washington State University, a public state university, the MBA admissions requirements include your Graduate Management Admission Test (GMAT) score, GPA (which must be above 3.0), and possession of a bachelor's degree.

- The admissions requirements for the MBA program at Pacific Lutheran University (a private nonprofit university) include transcripts from previous colleges, two references, GMAT or GRE scores, and a résumé.
- Application to Harvard Business School for an MBA requires a four-year undergraduate degree or its equivalent and your GMAT or GRE test scores.

If you plan to apply to one of these schools or a school with similar requirements, you would structure your undergraduate work to prepare you for the GMAT and/or the GRE. You would also focus on maintaining a high GPA and supporting any other goals necessary for graduate school admission.

BEYOND THE BIG THREE

As distance learning and online courses have grown in popularity over the past decade, more and more colleges have made this style of learning available. Currently, most colleges and universities offer either online courses or degrees completed online or both. Of 2,820 colleges surveyed in 2012, 86.5% offer online courses or complete online programs, with 62.4% offering complete online programs.[103] Here I list three colleges that have become associated with distance learning and that you may see mentioned on DegreeForum.net.

Kaplan University

Kaplan University, "a different school of thought," is regionally accredited through the Higher Learning Commission and has fourteen campuses in Indiana, Iowa, Maryland, Maine, Missouri, Nebraska, and Wisconsin. It was founded in 1937. Admission requirements include proof of high school graduation or GED and an enrollment agreement to be signed by a parent or legal guardian for students under 18.[104]

Students can use prior learning credits, including those from CLEP, DSST, AP, UExcel, and the military, for up to 75% of their degree (meaning the student must earn 30 credits from Kaplan University).[105]

Effective March 2, 2016, the per-credit tuition for undergraduate online programs is $371, which includes books and course materials.[106] After a student completes his final class and all requirements have been confirmed, a diploma will be mailed in approximately eight weeks. Commencement ceremonies occur at varying times each year across Kaplan campuses.

One notable course offered by Kaplan is their three-credit course entitled, "Documenting Your Experiences for College Credit."[107] This course carries ACE credit recommendation. The course is offered for free and teaches the student how to create a portfolio. If you create a portfolio using this class, you can submit it for credit by paying the appropriate fees. However, even if you do not create a portfolio, completing this class gives you three free credits that may be transferred to another school. (These credits would most likely be applied to your degree plan as electives; contact your school in advance of taking the class to determine exactly where these transferred credits would apply.)

Liberty University

Liberty University was founded in 1971 and is accredited through the Southern Association of Colleges and Schools Commission on Colleges. Liberty University is the largest private nonprofit university in America and the largest Christian university in the world, and their motto reflects their religious philosophy: "Training Champions for Christ." Admission requirements include sending your high school transcripts, an admissions essay, and your SAT or ACT scores.[108] Liberty University offers "The Edge," a dual enrollment program for high school junior and senior students, which has its own admission requirements.[109]

The per-credit cost for undergraduate online courses during 2016-2017 school year is $455 at the part-time rate (11 credit hours or less) and $390 for the full-time rate.[110]

The university accepts CLEP, DSST, and UExcel exams, and offers prior learning assessment. Students can earn up to 30 credits (31 for nursing students who hold their RN license) for prior learning, including credit-by-exam tests.[111] To earn an undergraduate degree from Liberty University, you must complete at least 50 percent of the major and 25 percent of the total degree through the University.[112] Degrees are granted throughout the year, and all graduates are invited to the annual commencement ceremony in May.

Liberty University offers a free Unofficial Transfer Consultation (UTC) to give you an estimation of how your transcripts will apply to one of their degree programs.[113] If you are a prospective Liberty University student and wish to see how your credits will be used toward a degree before applying to the university, this evaluation can be very helpful. Keep in mind that you will need to send transcripts of your credits (unofficial transcripts are accepted for the UTC), so the evaluation may not be entirely free if you need to pay for transcripts.

University of Phoenix

The University of Phoenix was founded in 1976 and is regionally accredited by the Higher Learning Commission. The University's mission statement is: "University of Phoenix provides access to higher education opportunities that enable students to develop knowledge and skills necessary to achieve their professional goals, improve the productivity of their organizations and provide leadership and service to their communities." As of March 2016, University of Phoenix has 112 campus locations that operate alongside the university's online programs.[114] To apply, you must have a "high school diploma, GED® equivalent, California High School Proficiency Examination certificate or foreign secondary school equivalent" and be at least 16 if applying to an associate degree program.[115] Some degree programs require the applicant to have specific licenses prior to admission.

A maximum of 30 credits from national testing programs (including AP, CLEP, DSST, and UExcel) can be transferred to the university and up to 54 community college credits may transfer.[116]

Online courses cost $410 per credit for 100/200-level courses and $610 per credit for 300/400-level courses.[117] Graduation ceremonies are held at various times during the year throughout the country.

Other Colleges

Degree Forum Wiki has a sample list called "Examples of Colleges Offering Distance Learning Courses" noting colleges offering low-cost online courses. The list includes a few important facts about each school, and can give you ideas of where to earn transferrable credit: http://degreeforum.wikia.com/wiki/Sources_of_Credit.

WHAT'S NEXT?

By narrowing your degree goals and collecting a short list of colleges to attend, you are now able to decide which degree and school will be your goal. Because of the time you spend identifying the unique nuances of both the degree and the school you choose, you will be able to plan your degree efficiently and utilize money-saving strategies throughout your degree journey. Even if you change your degree plan or school as you work toward your degree, your research will have simplified the available options to include only the degrees and schools most advantageous to you, making your new decision easier. The best part about choosing your degree major and school means you are now ready to craft your degree plan.

TAKEAWAY TIPS

- You can view quick facts about U.S. colleges at the National Center for Education Statistic's website: http://nces.ed.gov/collegenavigator/
- I wrote the following outline in my college journal to remind me of what was important for my degree major:

Choosing a degree means balancing:
1) What classes I want to take.
2) The amount of money spent on the degree: *Use credit-by-exams to reduce cost.*
3) The use of the degree after college: *How useful are the different degrees I am comparing?*

When I began looking for a major, I considered
- photography (fun, but difficult to complete using mostly credit-by-exam tests),
- food preparation (I would learn practical skills, but not in a field where I intended to pursue a career), and
- natural sciences/mathematics (a degree with opportunities to continue learning in some of the fields I enjoyed in high school).

In my senior year of college, I compared the natural sciences/mathematics degree with

- ○ business (useful for pursuing my goals of owning an online business),
- ○ history (fascinating and personally enriching), and
- ○ liberal arts (advantageous for the diversity of subjects I could study, but perhaps a less-impressive degree title).

4) Time spent on the degree: *I want to be done in four years.*

CHAPTER 11:

HOW TO MAKE A DEGREE PLAN

A degree plan is just like it sounds: a list of courses, credit-by-exam tests, and other college-level work that you intend to use to earn your degree. These credits are compiled so that they fulfill the degree plan you have chosen to complete. Having this list lets you schedule the order you will take courses/exams, track your progress toward your degree, and verify that your courses/exams are appropriate for the degree.

Creating a degree plan should be started before you enroll, shortly after you take your first few credit-by-exam tests (or sooner, if you know which degree you wish to pursue). To get started, you will need information about the degree found on the college's website and on DegreeForum.net. If you will be attending Charter Oak State College, Excelsior College, or Thomas Edison State University, you can benefit from DegreeForum.wikia.com, a website that hosts user-submitted outlines of the courses and tests that can be used to fulfill degree plans from the "Big Three."

Begin by finding the degree outline of your choice on the college's website. The federal government requires colleges that wish to be eligible for federal funding to make their programs and policies available to the public, and all six regional accreditors also require colleges to list their programs and policies publicly. Because of this, the degree outlines offered by a federally funded and/or regionally accredited college can typically be found on the college's website. You may find the outlines compiled under the academics section of the website or in the college catalog. The website's search feature can expedite locating them.

The degree outline will look similar to the three outlines of business degree concentrations shown in the last chapter, except that it will include not only the concentration but also the remaining courses which must be fulfilled to earn the degree. Now, we will match credit-by-exam tests and other distance learning methods to this outline to create your custom degree plan.

Degree Plan Mentoring

With the school's degree outline in hand, we now can select courses. It's important to note that besides choosing your degree and school and the actual learning required to reach your degree, creating your degree plan is the hardest part of the non-traditional degree journey. Posts pop up frequently on DegreeForum.net where students ask the forum gurus to look over their degree plan to fill in holes, identify errors, and offer money- and time-saving suggestions.

If crafting your degree plan seems daunting and you would rather pay someone instead of creating it yourself, consider signing up for CollegePlus. Creating a custom degree plan for you is one of the best features of CollegePlus, especially since this isn't the first time they have put together a degree plan—they know how to get you to your degree and how to steer you away from common pitfalls. CollegePlus has helped students earn credit toward degrees at over 100 colleges and universities.[118]

Another option for assistance with planning your degree is to use the services of Jay Cross, the founder of the Do-It-Yourself Degree program. He will create a customized degree plan for you and answer your questions as you complete the plan. His program costs $297, and you can visit his website for more information at www.doityourselfdegree.com.

However, even if you don't enroll with a mentor program like CollegePlus or Do-It-Yourself Degree, you don't have to plan your degree alone. Your resources are those mentioned in chapter 8: the internet, admissions counselors, and (once you enroll at your school) advisors.

A Brief Aside for Those Who Already
Have College Credit

If you have previously earned college credits, you can get a general idea of where your credits will fit in a particular degree by comparing the course identifiers of your credits to the identifiers listed in the course requirements. Additional information regarding transferring credits from a particular school or program can often be found by searching online.

One way to begin your degree plan when you have already earned credits is to send your transcripts to the college of your choosing and pay for an evaluation of the credits you have. Your transcripts can be from other colleges, the military, and credit-by-exam testing programs, to name a few. Depending on the college, evaluations are available before enrollment in two ways: by request (just send your transcripts to the college) or when you apply to the college. Both ways cost around $100 plus transcript fees. The evaluation shows how all the credits you have earned to date will apply to your degree. This way you can see exactly where your credits apply and which credits you have left to earn: a partially completed roadmap for earning your degree.

Do I Need an Evaluation?

You may choose to request an evaluation or apply if you are considering more than one college and want to see at which college your previously-earned credits are worth the most credit. Generally, requesting an evaluation before you are ready to enroll at the college of your choice is optional; the only time that an evaluation is crucial is if you have credits on a transcript that may dramatically affect your degree. If these credits in question will play a major role in your degree, such as fulfilling your core requirements, or if your decision of a major or even school hinges on the acceptance of certain credits, you will want an evaluation. On the other hand, if your transcripted credits are mainly lower-level or free elective credit, you will probably not need an evaluation before creating your degree plan. Plan your degree using these credits, knowing that if they are not accepted, you will need to replace the vacancies in your plan with other credits. These new credits could be from credit-by-exam tests, online courses, or other credit-earning opportunities.

CREATING A DEGREE PLAN

There are two paths to creating your degree outline, and the difference between the two is where you enroll. If you will be attending one of the Big Three, use the following steps. If you will be attending a college other than the Big Three, use the steps listed under "Creating a degree plan at a non-Big Three college." Both step-by-step guides assume you have chosen your degree and major and located the degree outline on the college's website.

Depending on your degree, you may be able to find a sample degree plan that already exists online. This saves you time and gives you a starting point to begin your degree plan research and customization. To find these degree outlines, say for a Bachelor of Science in General Studies, I suggest employing a search engine using the following keywords, "site:degreeforum.net Bachelor of Science in General Studies." To find other majors, replace "Bachelor of Science in General Studies" with the bachelor's degree you are searching for.

The other place to look for sample degree plans is http://degreeforum. wikia.com/. The Degree Forum Wiki plans are an excellent backbone for your degree plan. However, because the Big Three's policies change regularly, these plans should be considered templates and not patterns. Verify that the template you use corresponds to the current degree outline on the college's website. It can be wise to reference more than one template when creating your plan, pulling resources from many places.

An important component of degree plans is the course codes. The course code tells you which area of study the course is (business, English, nursing, etc.) and at what level (typically 100-299 are lower-level courses and 300-499 are upper level). These course identifiers are fairly straightforward to understand; BUS means business, PSY is short for psychology, etc. If you get stuck, use a chart like this one for explanations: http://www.tesu.edu/current-students/Course-Code-Descriptions.cfm.

Creating a Degree Plan at a Big Three College

How you create your degree plan will be affected by how many courses you want to test out of using credit-by-exam tests and how many you want to take using online courses. In this guide, I am assuming you want to take as many credit-by-exam tests as your degree will allow. Should you prefer less credit-by-exam testing, substituting online courses is a straightforward task.

Since I am most familiar with Thomas Edison State University, I will use a degree example from this school. Say you are interested in earning a Bachelor of Science in History. Begin with the degree outline page for the history degree.[119]

BA in History Credit Distribution

SUBJECT CATEGORY	CREDITS
I. General Education Requirements	60
A. Intellectual and Practical Skills	15
Written Communication	(6)
Oral Communication	(3)
Quantitative Literacy	(3)
Information Literacy	(3)
B. Civic and Global Learning	9
Diversity	(3)
Ethics	(3)
Civil Engagement	(3)
C. Knowledge of Human Cultures	12
D. Understanding the Physical and Natural World	4-7
E. General Education Electives	17-20
II. Area of Study: History	33
A. Required Courses	18
Western Civilization I & II (one year)	(6)
OR	
World History I & II (one year)	(6)
American History I & II(one year)	(6)
Non-Western/Non-U.S. History (e.g., Africa, Asia, Latin American, Middle East) (one semester)	(3)
Historical Methods/Historiography	(3)
B. Capstone	3
LIB-495 Liberal Arts Capstone	(3)

C. History Electives* African-American History American Labor History American Social History American Urban History Civil War and Reconstruction Classical Greece & Rome England in the Middle Ages History of Mexico History of New Jersey History of Religion History of the Vietnam War Male and Female in American History Modern Britain Modern France Modern Germany The American South The Cold War The Reformation The Renaissance The Supreme Court in American History War and Peace in the Nuclear Age	12
D. Requirements	
Courses transferred to Thomas Edison State University are equated to the following levels: 100, 200, 300 or 400. A minimum of 18 credits equating to 300 or 400 are required.	
III. Free Electives	27
Total	**120**

*This list is a guide. Other history courses may be appropriate for this area of study.

To commence filling in the degree plan, we will use a chart with course equivalencies. Equivalency charts tell us which credit-by-exam tests are equivalent to which courses at the university. The charts also give each exam's passing score and show whether an exam is worth upper- or lower-level credit. Most colleges host their unique charts on their website. For Thomas Edison State University, these equivalency charts can be found on pages 93-94 and 100-101 of the Undergraduate University Catalog (PDF version) here: http://www.tesu.edu/academics/catalog/index.cfm. The university catalog also lists TESU's available courses categorized by department.

There are two resources that can help you place credit-by-exam tests into your degree. The first, "General Education Courses: Enrolled in 2016 and After" page on Thomas Edison State University's website, shows which TESU courses and TECEP tests fulfill which general education requirements. (You can view the page here: http://www.tesu.edu/academics/courses/2016-and-After2.cfm.) This webpage will give you the course numbers and outline for plugging in CLEP tests.

The other resource is "Sanantone's TESU General Education Options After July 1, 2015" on Degree Forum Wiki: http://degreeforum.wikia.com/wiki/Sanantone's_TESC_General_Education_Options_After_July_1,_2015. Here, user Sanantone has compiled a list that includes not only credit-by-exam tests but other low-cost courses which are likely to satisfy these same requirements.

With these resources in hand, you can match CLEP exams to the degree requirements using the list of CLEP tests on the College Board's website (http://clep.collegeboard.org/exam) and TESU's CLEP credit equivalencies on page 100 in the Undergraduate University Catalog.

Repeat this matching process using DSST exams, utilizing DSST's exam list (http://getcollegecredit.com/exam_fact_sheets) and TESU's DSST credit equivalent chart on page 101 in the Undergraduate University Catalog (http://www.tesu.edu/academics/catalog/index.cfm).

With CLEP and DSST tests penciled into your degree plan, you will now see which credit requirements remain to be filled with TECEP exams, UExcel tests, other credit-by-exam tests, and/or online courses.

A few important notes about the following list:

1) Courses with no credit amount listed are worth three credits.

2) Courses/tests that are worth more than the amount specified for a particular requirement can be shared between different requirements; courses that are split between two requirements are placed in brackets when the remaining credits are used.

3) The courses shown are one example of how to fulfill these requirements. There is typically more than one way to arrange the same courses within a degree plan.

4) These are by no means the only courses you can use to fulfill a history degree. Use DegreeForum.net and the Degree Forum Wiki to view other options.

5) The website http://degreeforum.wikia.com/ has a collection of

user-submitted degree plans. Most plans are personalized and show the actual courses/tests that a student used to earn the degree, but there are a few sample plans that show various courses/tests that will fulfill degree requirements. These plans, especially those by DegreeForum.net user sanantone, provided the basis for the following sample.[120]

6) The university has the final say on where a course is applied within the degree plan. If you have questions on where your courses are applied, do ask for clarification from an admissions counselor or, if you are enrolled, from your advisor.

BA in History Credit Distribution

SUBJECT CATEGORY	TESU COURSE CODE	CREDIT-BY-EXAM TEST EQUIVALENTS	CREDITS
I. General Education Requirements			60
A. Intellectual and Practical Skills			15
Written Communication	ENC-101/102	• CLEP: College Composition—6 credits	(6)
Oral Communication	COM-209	• DSST: Principles of Public Speaking	(3)
Quantitative Literacy	MAT-121	• CLEP: College Algebra	(3)
Information Literacy	LIT-291	• CLEP: Analyzing and Interpreting Literature	(3)
B. Civic and Global Learning			9
Diversity	SOC-101	• CLEP Introductory Sociology	(3)
Ethics	PHI-287	• DSST: Ethics in America	(3)
Civil Engagement	POS-110	• CLEP: American Government	(3)

C. Knowledge of Human Cultures	PSY-211 ECO-111 ECO-112 SOS-305	• CLEP: Human Growth and Development • CLEP: Principles of Macroeconomics • CLEP: Principles of Microeconomics • DSST: Substance Abuse	12
D. Understanding the Physical and Natural World	NAS-101/102	• CLEP: Natural Sciences—6 credits	4-7
E. General Education Electives	MAT-102/103 HUM-101 PSY-101 SOS-101/102 HEA-103	• CLEP: College Mathematics • CLEP: Humanities • CLEP: Introductory Psychology • CLEP: Social Sciences and History—6 credits • DSST: Health & Human Development	17-20
II. Area of Study: History			33
A. Required Courses			18
Western Civilization I & II (one year)	HIS-101 HIS-102	• CLEP: Western Civilization I: Ancient Near East to 1648 • CLEP: Western Civilization II: 1648 to the Present	(6)
OR			
World History I & II (one year)			(6)
American History I & II (one year)	HIS-113 HIS-114	• CLEP: History of the United States I: Early Colonization to 1877 • CLEP: History of the United States II: 1865 to the Present	(6)
Non-Western/Non-U.S. History (e.g., Africa, Asia, Latin American, Middle East) (one semester)	HIS-351	• DSST: A History of the Vietnam War	(3)

Historical Methods/ Historiography		• See author's note.	(3)
B. Capstone			3
LIB-495 Liberal Arts Capstone	LIB-495	• TESU Online Course: Liberal Arts Capstone	(3)
C. History Electives* African-American History American Labor History American Social History American Urban History Civil War and Reconstruction Classical Greece & Rome England in the Middle Ages History of Mexico History of New Jersey History of Religion History of the Vietnam War Male and Female in American History Modern Britain Modern France Modern Germany The American South The Cold War The Reformation The Renaissance The Supreme Court in American History War and Peace in the Nuclear Age	HIS-399 HIS-315 HIS-310 Upper-level course	• UExcel: World Conflicts Since 1900 • Penn Foster: History of Labor in the United States • TESU Online Course: The Middle East • Ohio University Course Credit by Examination (CCE): Ancient Near East: Egypt, Mesopotamia, and the Levant	12

D. Requirements			
Courses transferred to Thomas Edison State University are equated to the following levels: 100, 200, 300 or 400. A minimum of 18 credits equating to 300 or 400 are required.		18 credits at 300 or 400 level.	
III. Free Electives	HIS-351	• DSST: A History of the Vietnam War	27
	COS-101	• CLEP: Information Systems	
	LIT-205	• CLEP: American Literature	
	LIT-208	• CLEP: English Literature	
	MAN-301	• CLEP: Principles of Management	
	MAR-301	• CLEP: Principles of Marketing	
	SPA-101	• CLEP: Spanish—6 credits	
	HIS-252	• DSST: The Civil War and Reconstruction	
Total			**120**

*This list is a guide. Other history courses may be appropriate for this area of study.

Author's notes: A) Several CLEP tests are currently worth six credits at TESU while ACE recommends only 3 credits. These titles are American Literature, Analyzing and Interpreting Literature, English Literature, and Humanities. Since I'm not sure how long these tests will be worth six credits, I've treated these titles as being worth 3 credits and filled in the remaining credits with other test titles. View the university catalog for the latest information. B) At the time of printing, I was unable to definitively determine which course(s) would fulfill this requirement. Since this degree plan was recently revised, more information should become available over time, or you may need to contact an admissions counselor or advisor.

CLEP tests not used in this degree plan: Biology, Calculus, Chemistry, College Composition Modular, Financial Accounting, Introductory Business Law, Introduction to Educational Psychology, Precalculus, French Language (Levels 1 and 2), German Language (Levels 1 and 2), and Spanish Language (Level 2).

More information about the Penn Foster course, History of Labor in the United States, can be found in the Penn Foster catalog (page 103): http://www. pennfoster.edu/college/catalog.

Information about the Ohio University exam, Ancient Near East: Egypt, Mesopotamia, and the Levant, can be found under the Course Credit by Examination (CCE) heading on this Ohio eCampus page: https://www.ohio.edu/ ecampus/print/course-list.html.

The most difficult part about this degree plan is finding 18 upper-level history concentration credits. However, there is an ever-changing number of online and credit-by-exam history courses, as courses are retired and new exams offered. Another upper-level course option mentioned on DegreeForum.net is a competency based exam (CBE) from Colorado State University- Global Campus, U.S. History from 1945 to the Present: https://csuglobal.edu/undergraduate/ programs/alternative-credit-options/cbes/.

Three options for free elective credit that are currently available at no charge include Kaplan's Documenting Your Experiences for College Credit course (3 credits), National Fire Academy courses (3 credits), and TEEX's Cybersecurity classes (6 credits).

Now for a few practical pointers for the other two schools of the Big Three:

If you are or will be attending Charter Oak State College:

- General Education Requirements: lists the groups of general education courses and shows how to fulfill each category. Some specific CLEP titles are named. http://www.charteroak.edu/ catalog/current/prog_study_degree_requirements/gen_ed_ requirements.cfm
- Credit Value of Specific Exams (PDF): shows credit-by-exam tests that are accepted by Charter Oak and gives the passing score, credit value, upper/lower level, and section of general education to which the exam belongs. Page with link to PDF: http://www. charteroak.edu/exams/list-of-exams.cfm.

If you are or will be attending Excelsior College:

- The Excelsior College Assessment-Based Degree: Excelsior College offers a plan for earning a Bachelor of Arts in Liberal Studies or in General Business for $10,000 or less (not including textbooks). This method includes the following benefits: a five-year time frame to complete the degree, access to an academic advisor, and six months to prepare for each exam.[121]

Creating a Degree Plan at a Non-Big Three College

Generally, you can use the same steps as listed earlier to create a degree outline at colleges other than the Big Three. Even though sample plans on DegreeForum.net for degrees from non-Big Three colleges aren't as easy to come by as those for degrees from the Big Three, it's always a good idea to search the forum for threads concerning the college you plan to attend. You never know how important just one tip from an alumnus can be.

One additional step you will need to do at a non-Big Three college is give extra scrutiny to the college's credit-by-exam test policy. Look for restrictions such as a maximum number of transferred credits, no upper-level credit awarded for credit-by-exam tests, credit-by-exam tests that only waive introductory courses and are non-credit bearing, and minimum credit-earning scores, as well as any other pertinent information you can find.

Begin with your degree outline. Because accredited colleges are required to make their degree plans available to the public, you can almost always find this outline online. Next, match required courses with the type of courses you wish to use (e.g., credit-by-exam tests, online courses, courses from your local community college, etc.). Make use of the course code identifiers as much as possible when matching courses.

How Do I Fill In and Verify My Degree Plan?

After a student has filled in their degree plan, how does the student know if they have completed it correctly? While some aspects of filling in a degree plan are relatively straightforward, verifying that the tests and courses you selected to fulfill the degree plan's requirements can be less than clear. Also, even if CLEP and DSST tests fit into a degree smoothly, it can be difficult to place other types of credit-bearing courses because they are challenging to compare with the courses recommended by the college.

There are two points here: how a student can find guidance when placing credits into a degree and what the student can do to verify that the degree plan is accurate. I address each in turn.

Placing Credits into a Degree Plan

For the student who is struggling to fulfill a certain course requirement or a certain section of courses, self-directed research can be an excellent option. Researching plans available online can demonstrate methods of achieving those same credits in a novel or unfamiliar way.

You will also want to make use of the extensive information available at DegreeForum.net. This information is especially targeted to these types of questions, so it is rare that you will be the first person to walk through a specific degree planning challenge. Make use of the site's search feature or use a search engine to query DegreeForum.net with the keywords of your questions.

As an example, if you can't find an upper-level mathematics test from CLEP or DSST and you are looking for other classes or programs to fulfill that course, search for just that: upper-level mathematics class. In my years using the forum, I've been pleasantly surprised by how regularly I've found posts from other students who needed, discovered, and shared a solution just like the one I was after.

Other options for help include requesting guidance on DegreeForum. net, with the warning that you are asking other students who are voluntarily providing you help, with no benefit or compensation to themselves. If you do request guidance, consider paying it forward and sharing your experiences, resource tips, and/or strategies to assist others on the forum.

If you are unable to locate an off-campus option that suits your degree, you can certainly request help from the college you plan to attend and explore the options they have on hand. Keep in mind that the college may not suggest self-directed learning options, so if that is your preference, you will want to ask specifically for credit-by-exam or off-campus courses.

If you've exhausted these free resources and are still doubtful enough of your plan that it is hindering your test-taking progress, it may be time to pay for mentoring.

Verifying Your Degree Plan

Once you've completed all or most of your degree plan, you are ready to double-check the outline you've created. Again, comparing your plan to those of others who have attended the same school you aim to attend will help immensely.

Another option that I have no experience using would be to email the college offering the degree to see if they will assist you. Of course, if you are enrolled, this service is included in your tuition, so do avail yourself of this opportunity. If you are postponing enrollment, you can still try contacting the college; I'm just unsure what help they will give.

THE RESULTS OF A DEGREE PLAN

Degree planning is challenging. This is one area where you have to work for the *thousands of dollars saved* by not going on campus. Regardless, you can still find success here even without 100% certainty in your self-made degree plan. Using my degree story, I will illustrate why.

Even by the end of my junior year of college, I didn't know if the plan I had created for myself would be accepted by TESU. I had compared my plan with degrees online, researched ad nauseam on DegreeForum.net, and referenced the degree planning material on TESU's website. Still, I was nervous about enrolling at TESU; what if not all of my credits transferred? What if I needed so many more credits that I had to take another year to study, ruining my chance to graduate in four years?

My pessimistic attitude was allayed only after I saw my evaluation of my credits. Hurray! They worked! There was only one class, DSST's Principles of Physical Science, that didn't apply in the degree's concentration as I planned when I took the course. The reason this course had to be moved was because I changed my degree plan from natural sciences/mathematics to social sciences. Even so, the exam still contributed to my degree as free elective credit.

Perhaps some of this uncertainty was warranted, but certainly not all. As an off-campus student, when you apply yourself to researching the requirements of a degree, when you take time to learn from students who have already earned their degree, and when you review and update your plan to reflect changes in school policy and your growing knowledge, you can combat pessimism with confidence.

This is especially true once you have chosen the general field of the degree you want to earn, as this gives you some flexibility within your degree field in the courses you select toward that degree. Only as the courses get more specialized and more specific (such as the courses taken in the senior year) will your course choices need to be quite accurate.

Happily, this is roughly the same time that you will be enrolling at your chosen school. Once you are enrolled, you will have an advisor who can answer your detailed questions, and an evaluation which will show you *exactly* where your credits will apply.

For all those pessimistic feelings and worries regarding the degree plan, there is the assurance that by including careful research, a flexible mindset, and a clear picture of your goals, you can confidently begin earning your general education credit. As you earn this credit, you will not only save money but learn the ropes of achieving a degree this way. Then, because of the background you now have with credit-by-exam tests, you can choose and earn upper-level credit, applying it to your degree with dexterity.

The Degree Plan Works for You

Planning your degree is one of the most significant aspects of the off-campus college experience. Knowing what a degree plan is and how it is developed allows you to target your efforts toward completing your degree. The plan becomes your roadmap. The roadmap shows you where you are, where you are going, and where you will be at the end of your journey. As you work out the fine details of your plan, keep these benefits in mind for motivation. Also, remember that a completely developed plan takes time. It may take several drafts before you have your final plan.

The most important thing to remember is to make your plan work for you. It is a tool. Creating the plan should not get in the way of taking credit-by-exam tests. In most degree plans from schools that accept credit-by-exam tests, you will be able to use the general CLEP exams somewhere in your degree. Continue with your credit-by-exam goals even as you refine your degree plan.

TAKEAWAY TIPS

- Creating a degree plan is a challenging part of the off-campus journey. Seek out advice from others, which can be found online, through the college, or from a third-party mentor, such as CollegePlus.
- To create your own personalized degree plan, remember this system:
  1) Find the appropriate degree outline on the website of the college granting the degree.

2) Decide how you prefer to earn your degree (credit-by-exam, online classes, community college classes, etc.).

3) To save money, use as many CLEP/DSST exams as your degree and your college allow.

4) Check for openings to use specialized learning methods (refer to chapter 6).

5) Search DegreeForum.net for specific tips for both your college and your degree.

6) Fill in the remaining courses with online courses or traditional classes, as necessary.

7) Look for updates to college policy, incentives, and specials offerings that are advantageous to you. Also, keep an eye out for other students working toward the same degree as you; they may provide you with innovative ways to gain credit for a certain course. Your degree plan will evolve as you complete courses and get closer to earning your degree.

8) Address questions to your advisor. (In select cases, an admissions counselor may be able to help you if you aren't enrolled.)

9) The college has the final say about which credits will be applied where. However, sometimes there is more than one place where credit can be applied; do ask for clarification about credit placement in your degree plan if you have questions.

CHAPTER 12:

SOCIALIZATION AND CREDENTIALING

The number one question I've been asked about earning a degree via distance learning is, "How are you going to meet people?" When my parents told acquaintances how my sister and I were completing college, the first question they were usually asked was also about socialization. These inquiries build on the assumption that earning a degree is more than just achieving a diploma or gaining education; it's also about making connections. The question for my parents includes the additional implication that socialization is something *parents* should foster for their children, including those of college age.

Over the four years I was earning my degree, I realized that beyond acknowledging the importance of socialization in college, many people feel that something inherent to pursuing a degree off campus is isolation from professors, other students, and even general acquaintances. As I began to work toward my degree, my friends and family were concerned for me—would I really experience the full breadth of the college experience if I didn't attend classes on campus? While it's true that the definition of distance learning says that the teacher and student are separated by distance or time, and sometimes both, the off-campus student is far from isolated.

Within questions of socialization lie several factors: What is the purpose of college beyond learning and earning a degree? How is the stereotypical college experience expected to help a student mature? Are there viable alternatives to the time-tested route of attending college on campus that include socialization? Does being off campus equate to being unsocial?

In my high school senior year, I was concerned that being off campus would limit my opportunities to be independent and to make new friends. I wanted to take responsibility for my higher education; did that mean I needed to live and study on my own? Would I require a professor to explain college-level material to me? Because these questions were so personal and their answers dependent on my personality and circumstances, I decided to give off-campus learning a one year trial to see if it would work for me.

Despite the fact that my family and I had researched and experienced enough non-traditional learning methods before college to feel confident in my decision to pursue at least a year of college off campus, we knew and told those who asked about distance learning that being off campus, especially earning a complete degree off campus, wouldn't work for everyone. But even though college without the campus isn't a panacea, it was the best way for me to reach my goals during my first year of college, and as it turned out, during the remaining three years as well.

In the end, non-traditional learning didn't hinder me from reaching my goals—it led me directly to them. I found that learning this way was complementary to my strengths. Along the way, I was able to verify that being off campus doesn't hold students back from socialization and that there are others interested in and motivated by learning off campus. These non-traditional methods are far more inclusive and usable than I ever dreamed before I started my own journey. Because of that journey, I not only earned my degree for under $10,000; I discovered what non-traditional learning truly offers to college students.

CAN A STUDENT RECEIVE THE SOCIAL BENEFITS OF COLLEGE WHILE OFF CAMPUS?

What about socialization off campus? How will a college student meet anyone new to expand her horizons if she is at home? These are important questions, because college and socialization have become so intertwined that they are often considered one and the same. College has become a way for young adults to create their own network of social contacts and to take on more independence and responsibility, and it has become a very common way to do so, with 68.4 percent of high school students attending college directly after graduation in 2014.[122] What is interesting but not surprising to note is that parents and students seem to have differing opinions about the objectives of college. Consider the following findings from the study of 2,322 students at 24 United States colleges and universities as presented in *Academically Adrift.*

What do parents want from college for their kids? They "want colleges to provide a safe environment where their children can mature, gain independence, and attain credentials that will help them be successful as adults."

What do students want from college for themselves? "Students in general seek to enjoy the benefits of a full collegiate experience that is focused as much on social life as on academic pursuits, while earning high marks in their courses with relatively little investment of effort."[123]

Indeed, as referenced in *Academically Adrift,* students who were interviewed by Rebekah Nathan, the author of *My Freshman Year,* saw "social activities and interpersonal relationships as the main context for learning."[124]

Taking into account the fact that the social side of college carries such importance (especially with students), we can respond to these findings in more than one way. We can view them as a reminder that alternatives to traditional college must still provide social opportunities in order for the traditional and non-traditional college experience to be comparable. This view may lead us to research the socialization avenues that are available through alternatives such as off-campus learning, online courses, or trade schools.

Another way we may view these findings is to recognize that though socialization is a factor of college equal to education, the college campus is not the only place and time to attain each. Socialization and education are separable. A student might choose to spend her precious time judiciously by studying alone, limiting socialization to maximize her progress. Then, she uses her free time for socialization.

The separation of studying and socializing still acknowledges the importance of each and even allows for varying amounts of time to be spent on both over the course of a year, term, or week. This separation isn't to say that these two must be mutually exclusive—occasionally combining the two can be motivating. However, by allotting specific time for socialization and study, the time spent on each has become more effective.

Making Friends

Friendships are a major component for college students, and it was certainly something I was concerned about going into college. Being on campus *is* a notable opportunity to meet people. Even though making new relationships isn't as simple as just being among other people, you do need to have people available to make friends with. So I wondered, would I be able to make new relationships off campus?

Knowing what I know now, I picture myself excitedly grabbing the shoulders of my former self and saying, "Of course!" People who haven't gone to college aren't friendless. People who are not in college but want to make new friends simply do so in other ways. I experienced this myself. Moreover, it turns out that making friends in college is not quite as it's popularly portrayed, regarding mixing with a diverse group of students from varying backgrounds and chance encounters that can turn into lifelong friendships.

While being on a college campus does surround you with potential friends, in *My Freshman Year*, author Rebekah Nathan notes that the majority of students' close relationships during college are with people met in their hometown or those that the student had met near the very beginning of college. The most significant college connections seem to come through meeting others living nearby (the same dorm, etc.) and through students who have similar demographics such as race, religion, and/or ethnicity rather than through meeting other students in the classroom.[125]

Even though we certainly can find friends in the classroom, off-campus students shouldn't feel that they are missing the exclusive opportunity for friendships by not being in a traditional classroom. Students should also realize that making friends on campus is not much different from making friends off campus.

Meeting People as an Off-Campus Student

If a student feels she would really benefit by meeting fellow students on campus, she may have that opportunity without enrolling in a traditional class. A sometimes-overlooked fact about credit-by-exam tests is that the testing centers are usually located on a college campus. Every time I took a DSST or CLEP test, I was among other students. Here was an occasion to meet people who were pursuing higher education. Being off campus the majority of the time does not close off opportunities for learning and meeting others. It merely changes how you encounter those opportunities. Furthermore, being off campus gives you options that were unavailable on campus.

Though on-campus students will most likely have easier access to college faculty and other college-related contacts, off-campus students still have access to a wide variety of people and may have more time to connect with these people, due to the off-campus student's mostly self-set schedule. Connections with business owners, advisors, office managers, parents, friends, and even local faculty may play a prominent role in your education. Certainly these same people are available for on-campus students, but off-campus students may have an easier time weaving these relationships into their learning.

Rather than missing out on opportunities to meet people, off-campus students will have the freedom to seek out others on their own terms. The most significant concept relating to the socialization of off-campus students is that the student realizes that she has control over the environment in which to make friends rather than letting the college set this environment. This concept extends beyond college. Making friends as an off-campus college student is another facet of non-traditional learning that prepares the student for life after college.

The Benefits of College Aren't Exclusive to the Campus

Spending less time on campus can help students remain in "the real world" and not be temporarily thrust into a reality removed from both life before college and life after college. This clearly challenges the "collegiate culture [that] emphasizes sociability and encourages students to have fun—to do all the things they have not had a chance to do before, or may not have a chance to do after they enter 'the real world' of the labor market."[126] While there are good things that can come of an experience that completely removes you from your ordinary way of life, there are many dangerous aspects of this method that can have large ramifications later.

Plus, many of the good things experienced at college are not available exclusively on campus. We've already talked about how the rubbing of minds can occur off campus, how meeting people isn't just an on-campus thing. By focusing on college as a means to your life goals, instead of the end goal, you can distill college to include the best preparation for life ahead. For me this included socialization, and so I found ways to include this element of college among my other goals.

MY SOCIALIZATION

Because my family and I had just moved from Pendleton, Oregon, to Walla Walla, Washington, the summer before I started college, I suppose it would have been possible for me to be isolated by becoming a hermit at my new house. However, moving to Walla Walla encouraged me to be the opposite of isolated. Here was a new community to explore and engage. I was continually encountering people and opportunities as I shopped, dined, patronized, worshiped, and learned.

And, although not many people I talked with knew about CLEP testing and fewer still knew of achieving a whole degree by testing out of classes, they were interested and usually excited to hear of another path to higher education, especially one that was so affordable. Rather than an isolation tactic, my choice of degree completion became an advantageous aid to introductions and conversations and a reminder for me to not be afraid to go against the flow.

Off-Campus Benefits

Students who choose to learn off-campus experience both positives and negatives; I was no exception. I was very thankful for the opportunity to work in my family's business, prepare to start my own jewelry and supplies business on Etsy, and spend time with my young cousins, along with other family members. Difficulties I faced were related to the responsibilities of earning a degree differently: learning to explain how I planned to earn my degree, answering questions about this method, and determining to not mind skepticism.

One problem that I didn't have was being the first to blaze this trail or being alone in using this style of learning. When I felt reluctant to continue studying, my mom would remind me of Brad Voeller and his successful journey. She would suggest I pull out his book for motivation. I also felt encouraged by the other students on DegreeForum.net and elsewhere who were completing their degree one credit-by-exam class at a time. These positive aspects helped me to keep moving ahead on my journey.

Another point that inspired me was that I had options I could choose from. Some of these options were available to me because of my family and their choices, but some of these options came directly from my attitude and my choices. I *chose* credit-by-exam testing: this gave me money to save and put toward other projects. I *chose* to be off campus: I found other ways to meet new people. It really wasn't so much the specific choices I had available that inspired me; it was the fact that I was making decisions for my life instead of letting other people and circumstances set my options for me.

Every educational endeavor has benefits and challenges. Earning a degree non-traditionally is not a cake walk. To pursue a degree this way requires certain resources, such as textbooks, internet access, and money for test fees. However, since every endeavor has obstacles, why not choose to overcome those obstacles that are on the road to your goals?

Off-Campus Challenges

One of the biggest difficulties I experienced while completing college off campus was evidencing progress toward my degree to people outside my immediate family. Unlike my on-campus counterparts, I didn't have the student ID card or college affiliation (or tuition bill!) to prove that I was going to college. Instead, my proof was my CLEP test scores and growing bank of college credits.

To effectively relate my degree journey to others, I had to complete a learning curve unrelated to my studies. I found that it was best not to affirm the suggestion that testing out of a class was like an online course because this insinuated college supervision and the involvement of a professor, and it misrepresented the nature of credit-by-exam testing. Basically, it confused people.

I also found that I needed to define the difference between passing a CLEP and passing a college course. I learned this the hard way: I ran into a friend and her friend on the Walla Walla University campus after I had completed the CLEP Calculus exam. "I just passed my calculus test!" I eagerly told them. I was baffled when their reactions didn't mirror my excitement;

they were baffled at my joy at passing a class. Only after my friend's friend said, "Well, I guess if you passed, that's all that matters," did I realize that two definitions of passing were preventing us from being on the same page.

Fortunately, once I better explained to others *how* I was doing what I was doing, people were able to understand that this was a viable way to earn a degree. I enjoyed being understood. I also enjoyed discovering that when off-campus learning has the chance to be explained sufficiently, more people can see its potential to benefit many different students.

For a deeper comparison of CLEP test scores and letter grades, see pages 165-66 in chapter 14.

Off-Campus Flexibility

What about students who either don't have a family of their own or don't want to live at home? I'm from a small town (Pendleton's population in 2010 was 16,612), and I know that many graduating high school seniors are ready to move on and move *out*. A typical sentiment my peers unflinchingly shared with me was that they could not wait to get out of town after graduation. Staying in town to go to school at the community college was certainly not as exciting or cool as rushing off to an out-of-town college, with the strains and pressures of being accepted, living without family, and discovering ways to finance the adventure.

Happily, the concept of distance learning can morph into different forms to fit many needs. Say you want to leave home and go on campus, but you'd like to save money and have a less rigid class schedule. Using credit-by-exam testing, you can earn college credit while still in high school, during summer breaks, or while you are on campus!

Even testing out of a couple of introductory courses will give you the flexibility to take more advanced classes earlier, to shorten the time spent on a degree, or to use the time you would have spent studying for those classes for other things, such as volunteer work, extracurricular activities, or, ironically, socialization. However you choose to use your free time, you will have learned the same concepts as you would have in class, but on your own time schedule, at a pace tailored to you.

On campus or off, education takes many forms, and utilizing these different study methods not only offers customization to the way a student learns, but it also gives the student a chance to cultivate skills that last throughout life. Let's discuss some of the ways education is changing and how socialization maintains its presence while changing along with education.

THREE FACETS OF EDUCATION

Sal Khan, author of *The One World Schoolhouse* and founder of Khan Academy, writes about three facets of education: teaching/learning, socialization, and credentialing, which can be defined as "giving a piece of paper to someone that proves to the world that they know what they know." He discusses the idea of separating the teaching and credentialing done by colleges.[127] Students would be free to learn at any college or through self-directed study, etc., and then take an assessment test where they would demonstrate their skills. In education and in the job world, Khan's idea moves the emphasis from *where* the student's learning was earned to *what* the student actually learned.

This is the very nature of credit-by-exam tests, and it is one way to infuse versatility into our present educational structure. As Sal Khan himself mentions, it is a way for students to not be limited by their age or their alma mater, but rather, what they have achieved in learning. He concludes his chapter about credentialing stating that this idea "would allow anyone, in any field, to better themselves and prepare for valuable credentials without the sacrifice of money and time that today's higher education demands."[128]

Khan's views on socialization include emphasis on age-mixed learning environments and peer-to-peer mentoring. Regarding age-mixed classrooms, he explains that when kids of different ages interact and learn together, both older and younger students are benefited. The older students are given responsibility to mentor and instruct, strengthening their understanding of the concepts they teach. The younger students have role models to emulate. He writes that "the schoolroom, rather than being an artificial cloister shut off from the rest of life, comes to more closely resemble the world beyond its walls—and therefore to better prepare students to function and to flourish in that world."[129]

Off-campus students can foster this same type of schoolroom by studying alongside siblings, peers, or mentors. Students of all ages can meet and study, even if they aren't all studying the same topic. This interaction provides the opportunity for explaining concepts to others and for the sharing of research strategies that can be used regardless of the topic.

As for peer-to-peer mentoring, this can be blended with age-mixed learning. As an off-campus student, you may meet with another family who has peers that are also in study mode. Or, you may join or create a local study group.

COLLEGE: A CHANGING LANDSCAPE

If the goal of education includes not only learning, but socialization and credentialing, then off-campus learning must fulfill all three attributes. For socialization, the off-campus student allocates time and seeks out places to connect with others, form relationships, and build friendships. This is a skill that will reside in the student for life.

Credentialing is evolving all the time. Right now there are many ways to earn credit without the campus, including credit-by-exam testing, online courses, and off-campus internships. More and more colleges are offering open courses, and some are even offering credit-bearing certificates upon completion. These small steps could be leading us to a future that accomplishes Sal Khan's vision of focusing on what you have learned, rather than where. We are already seeing these changes begin.

We can be excited by these changes. Perceptions of college are shifting, especially as we note that socialization, though an integral part of college, can occur off campus successfully. Separating meeting people from the college campus as well as separating the credentialing function of colleges from teaching are just two of the ways that the college landscape is changing.

Most exciting are the findings that many students are benefiting from the bevy of learning methods available. These methods not only bring education to more people, they also encourage students to take charge of their own learning and develop skills they can use throughout their life.

Above college's more measurable objectives, like sharing knowledge, creating an environment for socialization, and approving degrees, teaching students how to learn is the highest achievement of both college and education. For individuals with this skill, even socialization becomes an attribute that can be practiced and *learned.*

TAKEAWAY TIPS

- Be prepared to educate others about the opportunities for socialization that exist off campus. Giving an example of how you are meeting people can help them see beyond the misconception that all meaningful socialization stems from a college campus.
- Making friends can happen anywhere.
- There are some trade-offs for any method of pursuing college. However, in the case of college off campus, the trade-offs are a small price to pay to complete college with flexibility and opportunities for self-directed and self-paced learning.

CHAPTER 13:

PREPARING FOR LIFE AFTER COLLEGE

When I began my degree journey as an optimistic and resolute eighteen-year-old, I had great hopes for my college experience. I didn't know exactly how far college off campus would carry me, but I knew it would help me get started toward my degree. My goal was simple: I wanted to earn my degree in three years without debt. Completing my general education credits through CLEP testing would certainly start me down the right path.

As I went along, I had to modify my time frame to accommodate my goals outside of college. Unless it was absolutely necessary, I didn't study when my family entertained guests or when we went on vacation. I also enjoyed watching one or two TV programs during the week, along with a family movie on the weekend. I took time to help in my family's business, connect with family and friends, and try new things.

My degree time frame stretched to four years because of three reasons: I put family and some leisure activities before study, switched my degree major, and changed my preference of online courses (which I had planned to postpone until I enrolled near the end of my degree) to credit-by-exam tests (which I could have taken anytime). Fortunately, I didn't pay tuition until my fourth year of college anyway, so these modifications didn't add to the degree's price tag.

This was another instance where I *chose* to include these family and recreational activities during college; family was (and is) just as important as my learning, and recreation helped me be well-rounded. However, I made sure to not let family engagements and activities obstruct my progress.

Brad Voeller reserves a whole chapter in his book for the topic of achieving maximum efficiency, and in it he mentions what he calls "time robbers" such as TV, surfing the internet, and videos. (Shall we add texting to the list?) With his track record of a bachelor's degree in six months, Brad Voeller is certainly qualified to give such advice. Voeller says, "When I was pursuing my degree, I only watched half of one video that was unrelated to my studies. Why stare at a video when you could be speeding toward your degree?"

Even when taking a more moderate approach, it's critical to use our precious time in such a way that it benefits our goals. Harmonizing study within everyday life *during* college is great preparation for balancing family, friends, working, resting, socializing, and personal time within everyday life *after* college. The need for juggling opposing forces hasn't diminished in recent years; we have an ever-evolving array of distractions that require us to work smarter. By strengthening our study skills and our balancing skills, we do just that.

Credit-by-Exam Tests and Swiss Cheese Learning

There is hardly a better way to hone these study skills than by tackling a few credit-by-exam tests such as those from CLEP. CLEP tests are a test of endurance and determination as well as knowledge. The endurance required isn't just for sweating out the 90 minutes of the test; it's for studying persistently, forgoing hobby projects and coffee dates. It's for acquiring effective study tools like speed reading and memory techniques. It's for learning to keep yourself motivated and for surrounding yourself with a support team.

There are two aspects of CLEP tests and other credit-by-exam tests that must be overcome for this learning method to be successful. The first is maintaining self-directed accountability. I've mentioned some of my tips for staying motivated, and we've discussed how to reach out for help from admissions councilors, advisors, family, and other students.

The remaining aspect of credit-by-exam testing is becoming knowledgeable about this method's legitimacy. This includes answering questions such as: Will students actually learn anything from studying and then taking a test like CLEP? Will "learning to a test" result in insufficient knowledge about a particular topic? What if students cram information, walk into a test room, take the test, and then forget everything they've learned? This sounds like an inherent problem that is specific to the credit-by-exam method, but the same process can happen with any method of learning. We study for what we need to know, after which we forget the information we don't use and review.

There is a danger with all types of learning for the student to come away with what Sal Khan calls "Swiss cheese learning." This happens when a student learns a subject without mastery. The student absorbs enough information to achieve 75-80 percent on a final test and then moves on. The hazard here is that when the student tries to build on his knowledge, he will reach a point where he needs that information that he didn't fully grasp: the information needed for that last 20-25 percent. The student cannot continue learning until he fills in these holes.[130]

Swiss cheese learning also occurs due to memory attrition. Over time, even things we know well tend to fade. Thus, we may need to fill in holes in our learning before we can build upon what we know currently. Because the mastery of a subject is not a static state, the tools we develop to aid self-directed learning are valuable for not only the time spent earning a degree, but for life.

Jeffrey Selingo, a contributing editor to *The Chronicle of Higher Education* and author of *College (Un)Bound,* actively researches and reports about higher education, the employment of graduates, and changes in the structure of college. He says, "Overall, I have found by talking to employers and educators that what they want most in their workers is the ability to learn how to learn. In other words, the capability to find the answers to the questions of tomorrow that we cannot envision asking today."[131]

It would be difficult for me to overestimate how much studying for my degree helped me write and research this book. This is significant since I didn't seriously consider writing a book about my college experience until late in my college senior year, so I didn't choose my degree or classes with writing in mind. Yet, I had the skills I needed, such as using a search engine rigorously, transferring thoughts to paper, and, most crucially, directing my attention to a project diligently. My book writing project used the same techniques I practiced throughout my degree: the skills of how to learn.

When these skills are emphasized and exercised during college, regardless of your degree major, you have a background that will aid you no matter what you decide to learn or do next. These abilities are the degree's fundamental value: your degree is preparing you for *life* ahead, not just for one job or one field. The degree's rootedness in real life keeps the skills you learn suited for real life as well.

"Learning is important because we are changed by what we learn, even if the facts are later forgotten. Learning changes values, attitudes, and concepts that don't fade in time." ~Dr. James Dobson, The New Dare to Discipline, *p.195.*

Motivational Education

Directing your own education requires discipline and basic resources (like time, money, and information). While off-campus learning is not something everyone enjoys, it has a broader appeal than we might think. More students can tackle this method of learning than we've been led to believe. Sal Khan wrote about this. When he first began creating videos for what would become Khan Academy, he thought the videos would be watched by a select group of students. He was not alone in holding this view; other people felt that perhaps only 20 percent of students would succeed using videos to improve their learning. After all, only a small group of students are motivated by learning in a self-directed manner, right?[132]

As Khan Academy has grown and aged, Sal Khan has seen proof of the opposite. He found that students who had been given up on by others and who had nearly given up themselves were able to turn their education around by taking charge of their own learning. Seeing these students succeed gave Sal Khan a new perspective. He writes, "It made me realize that if you give students the opportunity to learn deeply and to see the magic of the universe around them, almost everyone will be motivated."[133]

The best learning takes place when students have a personal stake in their education. Students today can pull from as many or as few resources as preferred, and they can decide whether to study only to pass the test or to continue toward mastery of that topic. Should students find later that they didn't dig deeply enough into a subject, they can use their customized study habits to easily revisit the subject for a refresher or deeper inquiry.

Land, Ho!

When I earned the last credit of my degree by completing a DSST test, I was elated to have finished my degree. Receiving my diploma in the mail a few months later was a highlight of completing college. I had reached my goal!

I began my degree as an optimistic 18-year-old; four years later, as a still optimistic 22-year-old, I celebrated the accomplishment of my degree while I continued toward ongoing goals, and I smoothly transitioned into other projects, including opening an Etsy store. My skills of "learning to learn" kicked into gear as I navigated starting and running my own online shop. Being able to easily move from a focus on study and higher education to entrepreneurial and literary pursuits was a blessing and a welcome outcome of my college without the campus experience.

As you continue your own educational journey, may you set goals and see them realized *throughout* your college journey. May your education provide you with skills that support your life aspirations. Above these, may you love learning. I wish you success!

TAKEAWAY TIPS

- Learning how to teach yourself will benefit you throughout life: this skill is a remedy for Swiss cheese learning and memory attrition.
- Employ off-campus college techniques to assist you in reaching your goals!

CHAPTER 14:

FREQUENTLY ASKED QUESTIONS

FAQS FOR THE INTRODUCTION & CHAPTER 1: WHY COLLEGE?

Q: What is off-campus college?

A: Off-campus college is a method of gaining college-level education with a focus on self-directed learning. This method can be used to earn part or all of a degree. Course requirements can be completed through credit-by-exam testing, online courses, a demonstration of life experience (like prior learning assessment), and free or open classes (such as massive open online courses).

Q: What is credit-by-exam testing?

A: This is a method for students to demonstrate what they have learned, regardless of where their learning comes from. To gain the knowledge necessary for the test, students can study on their own, take a not-for-credit class, complete a textbook, and/or pull from their practical experience acquired from life or on the job. Then, students register and take the test. If a passing score is achieved, students send their score to the college(s) of their choice. It is typical for a test provider to keep students' scores on file for twenty years.

Q: What is distance learning?

A: Distance learning is learning that consists of the teacher and student being separated by time or distance, or both. It can take many forms, including online classes, correspondence courses, massive open online courses (MOOCs), and web conferencing.

Q: Hillary, how is the way you took courses different than taking online classes?

A: The main difference between credit-by-exam testing and online courses is the lack of a professor to guide you in the credit-by-exam method. Credit-by-exam courses put the burden of learning upon the student. However, this doesn't mean that the student is alone in learning: the student has the opportunity to select resources and advisors as needed. The structure of online courses parallels a traditional college course, including a specified textbook to learn from and interaction with a professor and other students.

Q: What is the difference between semester credit hours and quarter credit hours, and how do I convert one to the other?

A: Semester and quarter credit hours are both ways to report students' work throughout the year. The difference between the two is how the year is divided: into three sections (semesters), or into four sections (quarters). Each college decides which credit hour system they will use.

   If you plan to transfer credit from a school on the semester system to a school on the quarter system, or vice versa, you will want to know how many credits your work will be worth. To convert semester credit hours to quarter credit hours, multiply semester credits by 1.5. To convert quarter credit hours to semester credit hours, multiply quarter credits by 0.667.

FAQS FOR CHAPTER 2: THE FINISH LINE & CHAPTER 3: FEES AND TACTICS

Q: *How does college debt affect a student in the long run?*

A: First we must recognize that college debt can be acquired to fund not just tuition, but a particular lifestyle. "Students do not view debt exclusively as an investment, but also as a vehicle for consumption."[134] Using debt, students can move out from home, join clubs that require monetary resources, and work less. Many students feel justified in utilizing debt because of the perceived freedom that this money provides: freedom to fully embrace the college experience. However, the consequences of this debt can affect the student for years.

In the same paper quoted above, the authors suggest that college debt affects when a person marries and has children. They also more strongly suggest that debt has an effect on buying a home and a car.[135] In 2014, *The New York Times* published a piece entitled, "The Ripple Effects of Rising Student Debt," corroborating the influence of debt on home buying. They highlight research showing that people with student loans are less likely to purchase a home as well as start their own business.[136] In a Pew Research study, it was found that the median net worth ($64,700) of households headed by a young college-educated adult with no student debt was seven times greater than median net worth ($8,700) of households headed by an adult with student debt.[137]

Student loan debt has also been found to negatively affect individuals' physical well-being and sense of purpose.[138] In 2014, Gallup-Purdue released a report studying more than 30,000 college graduates across the United States. In this index, well-being was separated into five aspects: purpose, social, financial, community, and physical. Debt negatively affected all five.[139]

Q: *What about financial aid for distance learners?*

A: Student financial aid is available through three sources: from the government at both the federal and state levels, from colleges and universities directly, and from private parties. The main criterion for a distance learner to receive financial aid is if the student is enrolled. This is understandable, since it is easier to ensure that the aid is used as intended if a student is enrolled.

For aid from the federal government, students are required to be enrolled at an accredited institution.[140] Thus, once a student enrolls, she will be eligible for funding regardless of whether she attends on campus or off campus. The same is true for aid from state governments, from colleges and universities directly, and from most—if not all—private organizations. Once the students enroll, they are eligible for aid. The good news for unenrolled, off-campus students is that the reasonable fees of non-traditional learning can preclude the need for financial aid.

FAQS FOR CHAPTER 4: INTRODUCING CLEP TESTS & CHAPTER 5: MEET DSST TESTS

Q: Where can I expect to have my exam proctored?

A: Many credit-by-exam tests are administered at a college campus. While the testing location requirements vary with each brand of test, many of the basic test criteria are met through an on-campus facility. Colleges are equipped with the computers, proctors, and credentials to administer tests, making them a likely place for taking credit-by-exam tests. Off-campus testers can use this to their advantage by visiting their hometown college's website to learn what types of tests are already offered.

Because several of the large testing companies develop and administer more than one brand of test, there is overlap in where and how tests are administered. This means that if a college is equipped to offer CLEP tests, they may be able to conveniently proctor other types of tests you plan to take. Therefore, it is wise to approach a local college about becoming certified to proctor additional tests accepted by the college you will be attending.

Q: I live in a small town. Who will proctor my test?

A: Even if you live in a very small town, you may be able to find someone who meets the criteria to proctor tests. You can usually find the proctor criteria on the test sponsor's homepage.

If there isn't a testing center or someone qualified to give your test locally, consider nearby cities. During my years in high school, there wasn't a CLEP test provider or proctor established in Pendleton, but I was surprised to find that there were three CLEP testing locations that were each about an hour's drive away.

Q: Hillary, how many tests did you take overall?

A: I took the following number of tests: CLEP, 17; DSST, 10; FEMA courses, 19; for a grand total of 46 tests.

Q: What can I expect from my CLEP test credits?

A: The worst outcome is that you would not be able to use any of your CLEP credits toward your degree (perhaps you change your mind about enrolling at a college that accepts CLEP, or you decide not to go to college). The most probable outcome is that you would be able to use most or all of your CLEP credits, even if they apply in the free elective section (maybe you changed degree majors during your study). The best outcome is that you could use your CLEP credits to test out of two years' worth of college classes!

Q: I just completed a CLEP test. Even though I earned a credit-earning score, I'm disappointed that I didn't earn a better score!

A: After my initial exhilaration of completing a test wore off, another feeling immediately followed: a feeling of inadequacy. I was upset that I didn't ace the test! I had put time and effort toward completing this test, so why didn't this show in the form of a perfect score?

My disappointment stemmed from comparing a credit-by-exam test to the final of a college class. The following chart shows why this is not a relevant comparison:

	CLEP TEST	FINAL OF A COLLEGE CLASS
Preparation	Several suggested resources	Specified resources and a professor who can tell you what information will be covered by the test
Grading system	Pass/fail	Letter grades
Benefit from earning a perfect score or an A	None	Good grades, which affect GPA

Here are some key points to remember if you are feeling frustrated about your credit-by-exam test score:

- Knowing what information will be on a credit-by-exam test can be more difficult than knowing what information will be on a final exam. Textbooks and other resources can be more numerous and varied than those for a college class. This makes it a challenge to study for a perfect score.

- "Passing a credit-by-exam test" is not the same as "passing a class."
- You may see some students who relate CLEP scores to letter grades. This is a holdover from years ago when Excelsior College did assign letter grades to transferred CLEP credit. While the College Board has released B-level scores for CLEP tests,[141] few schools assign letter grades to CLEP scores at this time.
- Scores do not equate to percentages. CLEP test scores, for example, fall between 20 and 80; this means that earning a score of 60 is not the same as answering 60% of the questions correctly. When you take a CLEP test, you receive one point for each question answered correctly with no points deducted for questions answered incorrectly. Points from questions answered correctly are totaled, and then converted to a scaled scored between 20 and 80. According to College Board, scores are scaled to keep scores consistent between different test forms and to ensure that your score does not depend on how others scored on the same test as you.
- Scores from different CLEP tests do not relate to each other.

For more information, see the What Your Score Means document at http://clep. collegeboard.org/about/score.

Q: Do DSST tests have letter grade equivalents?

A: While DSST tests are also scored as pass/fail, DSST test scores do directly relate to letter grades given in a corresponding college course. Earning a passing score on a DSST test is equal to achieving a grade of C. You can also find scores equivalent to a B-grade listed on the data sheet available on the webpage listed below. Depending on whether the exam has been refreshed (updated), the tests are scored from 200-500, with a passing score of 400; or 20-80, with passing scores between 44 and 49. The B-grade equivalent for tests with a three-digit score is 434, while the B-grade equivalent for tests with a two-digit score ranges from 48-55.

What does this mean for the student who takes DSST tests? Not much, since most schools *do not* award letter grades. If you complete the test with a credit-earning score, you will receive credit. Thus, the key points in the previous Frequently Asked Question regarding CLEP test scores hold true for DSST test scores as well.

You can find more information about DSST scores in the Technical Data Sheet available here: http://getcollegecredit.com/exam_fact_sheets.

Q: Which schools take CLEP/DSST?

A: This information is available on the College Board's website for CLEP and the GetCollegeCredit website for DSST. Although this information is generally accurate, verify the policies of the school you plan to attend *before you take a test* to be sure they will accept that test.

CLEP: http://clep.collegeboard.org/search/colleges
DSST: http://getcollegecredit.com/institutions/search/

Q: I'm going to take a CLEP (or DSST) test. I think I'm going to attend College Z, but I'm not enrolled. On the day of testing, should I send my test score to College Z?

A: It depends. Check College Z's policy on sending your test score before enrollment. Some colleges keep your score on file for six months or so before they shred that information. What is the advantage of sending your score to the college before you enroll? Well, if you have the score sent to the college at the time of testing, the score is sent for free. If you don't send the score at the time of testing, you will need to pay $20 to have all your CLEP scores (or $30 for DSST scores) sent to the college.

On one hand, if you don't think you will enroll within 6 months to a year, you may want to hold off from sending your score. On the other hand, you might want to send your score anyway—and save $20 if you happen to enroll earlier than you planned.

Q: Which CLEP test should I start with?

A: For your first CLEP test, choosing a subject you enjoy is always a good idea. Also, choosing a test in which you learn and practice skills that you will be using later is handy. I will risk throwing out a few specific CLEP titles, but do consider other CLEP titles that play to your strengths.

Analyzing and Interpreting Literature–Do you enjoy reading and answering questions about what you read? You might find this a breezy way to earn three credits.

College Composition–Enjoy writing essays? If you know how to coherently put your thoughts on paper or you want to develop this skill, taking this test first or early in college will strengthen your prose for other writing assignments throughout college. If writing is not your strong point, this would still be an okay first test; just allow yourself plenty of time to prepare. College Composition is a six-credit test.

Language tests–While I strongly feel that a language test is not the best first test for those who are just learning a language, a language test can be the perfect first test for fluent speakers. You can earn up to nine credits.

Principles of Management–Since I haven't taken this test, I mention it based only on reviews I've read. Not surprisingly, it seems to be an easier test for students with management experience or background. The test is worth three credits.

Q: Which CLEP tests are recommended by the American Council on Education (ACE) to be worth six credits?

A: • Biology
  • Chemistry
  • College Composition
  • College Mathematics
  • Natural Sciences
  • Social Sciences and History
  • French, German, and Spanish language tests, worth six or nine credits, depending on your score.

Q: Should I take CLEP's College Composition or College Composition Modular?

A: It depends on how many credits you want to earn and which college you are transferring the test to. The American Council on Education recommends six credits for College Composition and three credits for College Composition Modular *without* the optional essay portion and six credits *with* the essay portion.

Colleges will usually specify on their website which composition test they accept or prefer and how many credits each test is worth. For example, TESU's CLEP page in the Undergraduate University Catalog shows that TESU does not prefer one test over the other (both tests are accepted) and that College Composition is worth six credits, while Modular is worth three credits.[142]

Q: I've figured out which CLEP/DSST exams I need to take; how do I know in what order to take them?

A: While CLEP and DSST tests span several subject areas, there are enough tests with related material that you can benefit from grouping tests with similar content. The Free-Clep-Prep website has a CLEP and DSST Overlap List showing the tests arranged into specific content categories sorted by difficulty. If you want to see a list of just CLEP exams arranged from least to most difficult, check out Free-Clep-Prep's CLEP Difficulty List.[143]

Q: How many CLEP and DSST tests should I study for at once?

A: This is a great question to answer at the beginning of your college study. It is also a great question to revisit periodically. The number of subjects you study will largely depend on your personal study habits, your time allotment for degree completion, and your motivation level.

When I started my degree, I had experience with two styles of learning: the unit study approach and the more typical semester-style approach. In the unit study method, you intensively study one subject for a specified period, say four weeks. Because you are directing all your effort toward one subject, you will have a chance to study it from different angles. This can be fun. You might take a field trip, do hands-on experiments, write a paper, or watch a video lecture series, all the while tailoring these activities to a single subject. Downsides to this approach include getting tired of studying that particular subject before you have learned the necessary information and not finishing the subject within your designated time frame.

Taking a more longitudinal, semester-style approach to study might mean studying four subjects per semester, for a total of eight subjects per school year. In this method, you enjoy the diversity of studying many subjects concurrently. You can still include fun projects and field trips in this style of learning; now you will have different activities for different subjects scattered throughout the year. Potential pitfalls include being spread too thin and not achieving the depth of study required for each subject. Another consideration is that the tests for all the subjects occur at the same time rather than being staggered over the course of the year.

Q: Can I use a college textbook to study for a CLEP or DSST test?

A: Yes! CLEP and DSST's test creators even offer textbook suggestions. The College Board's textbook examples are located online in the Study Resources for each exam. DSST textbook resources are listed on the test's Fact Sheet.

Because most CLEP and DSST tests cover general education, many commonly-available textbooks for the test's topic will cover the same material as the test. You can compare the textbook's content outline with the content of the CLEP/DSST test to determine if the textbook is suitable study material.

Q: How do I determine parameters for my study, and how do I know when I've studied enough?

A: This is a difficult aspect of credit-by-exam testing; however, with each test you take, you have more experience to gauge this for yourself. The three things that helped me know that I was studying relevant information were the test outline from the test creator, pretests, and the Exam Specific threads on DegreeForum.net.

The test outline is the number one source to help you choose the resources you will use because it shows how much emphasis the test will place on individual subject areas. Pretests, especially those from the test creator, will indicate if you are studying the right topics and give you ideas of concepts to review. After you take around three tests, you will learn how your practice test scores translate to actual test scores, and how familiar you need to be with a subject to be comfortable in the test room.

The Exam Specific thread can help you pinpoint how ready you are to test. You'll find practical suggestions such as: Did you nearly ace Peterson's practice test? You're probably ready to test because Peterson's practice test for this subject is harder than the actual exam. Have you extensively studied topic X? Good, because the test focuses on it.

Q: Hillary, how long did you prepare for a CLEP test?

A: For CLEP Spanish, several years. Some of my more difficult subjects took half the school year. Easier subjects or subjects that I had some background in took about one or two months each.

Q: *What is the brain dump technique?*

A: This is a testing technique with several interpretations. One definition applies to tests where scratch paper is provided or where writing in the test booklet is allowed. The student crams as much information into her memory as she can before entering the testing room. Once the test has started, the student writes this information from memory onto her scratch paper for use during the test. I employed this technique with a strong emphasis on putting the information to memory during my study in the *weeks* leading up to the test, rather than the *minutes* leading up to it.

Another definition of the brain dump technique is where the student takes 3-5 minutes before a test to dump all negative thoughts from the mind by writing them on a piece of paper. By removing these thoughts, the student frees up the brain's working memory to concentrate on the test rather than worries.

Thanks to its various forms, the brain dump technique can be useful for many students in different situations. Whether it is by writing down test-related information for the comfort of having a set of facts or formulas on a paper in front of you, or by purging negative thoughts from your mind, this technique is a great way to settle testing nerves and restore confidence in your knowledge.

Q: *What are the Exam Specific threads on DegreeForum.net?*

A: These threads are online conversations about a specific topic with one thread designated for discussing an individual test title. Each thread contains resources that students found helpful when preparing for the test. Users also share which practice tests they used, how their practice test scores related to their actual test scores, and how they would prepare differently if they were to take the test again. Because these threads are so informative, you may decide to enroll with InstantCert for access to the Exam Specific section of the DegreeForum.net even if you aren't using InstantCert's flashcards!

Q: *You refer to DegreeForum.net a lot. Why do you recommend this resource so strongly? Are you receiving a commission?*

A: I recommend DegreeForum.net because besides Brad Voeller's *Accelerated Distance Learning*, DegreeForum.net was my number one resource throughout my college journey. I thrived on having a website where I could unobtrusively learn how to earn my degree. I could research my questions at any time of day. I could find others who had overcome the same hurdles I was facing. And, I could be inspired to keep studying when I didn't want to.

Another reason I recommend DegreeForum.net is that new information is added daily. DegreeForum.net helps me keep updated on the Big Three's changes in policy and allows me to learn from other people excited to be earning their degree as self-directed students.

I don't receive compensation from DegreeForum.net. To my knowledge DegreeForum.net doesn't pay users to promote the site.

FAQS FOR CHAPTER 6: SPECIALIZED LEARNING METHODS

Q: I have musical or other skills that are at the college level. Is prior learning assessment (PLA) worth looking into to demonstrate my learning and earn credit?

A: If your credit potential is worth the risk of putting together a portfolio and not receiving credit for it, then certainly find out more regarding PLA! In fact, the following link tells how one student used PLA to earn 24 upper-level music credits. Bear in mind that she wrote over 80 pages to document her learning, and that the PLA portfolio prices and the number of credits earned per portfolio have changed.

http://www.degreeforum.net/general-education-testing-discussion/21129-learning-counts-pla-update.html

Q: What are my options for completing PLA-100 and PLA-200 (the classes required for prior learning assessment [PLA] and portfolio creation at TESU)?

A: PLA-100 is a one-credit, four-week course that prepares the student to earn credit through the PLA portfolio process. PLA-200, an eight-week course worth two credits, walks the student through the actual process of putting together a portfolio. Both courses are offered directly from TESU,[144] and can be completed once you enroll. An alternate route is to complete the open version of these two courses, which are available for free. However, when the two PLA courses are completed in this way, they are not eligible for credit at TESU. Completion of the open courses does allow you to submit portfolios to TESU.[145]

You may also complete an equivalent PLA course at another college or via an open course such as the one available from Kaplan,[146] and then be eligible to submit portfolios for credit. These courses may require you to enroll or they may be free, and they may or may not be credit-bearing.

For more information about the TESU PLA process, visit: www.tesu.edu/pla.

Q: What off-campus options are available for classes like biology with lab?

A: There are online courses for classes like these. Lab projects can be completed off campus using a kit and verified by sending pictures and reports to your instructor. The course cost varies, and by looking into programs at different schools, you can compare prices of equivalent courses. For more information about this, view the following threads on DegreeForum.net, and search the forum and online: http://www.degreeforum.net/general-education-testing-discussion/15334-science-college-course-programs-available-online.html

http://www.degreeforum.net/excelsior-thomas-edison-charter-oak-specific/21636-science-lab.html

Q: What are some other online websites where I can find free resources?

A: Besides the MOOC websites and MOOC aggregators listed under "Massive Open Online Course" in chapter 6, here are a few additional websites listing free courses and resources:
http://www.collegeaffordabilityguide.org/college-for-free/moocs-that-offer-credit-by-exam/
http://www.hippocampus.org/
http://www.ocwconsortium.org/
http://www.oercommons.org/
http://www.opencourselibrary.org/

FAQS FOR CHAPTER 7: MOTIVATION

Q: Hillary, what was your schedule like during college?

A: Though my routine looked different over the four years of my degree, my basic agenda stayed similar. This was my target schedule, and the closer I followed it, the more I achieved.

7:30 a.m. Rise, prepare for the day and eat breakfast.

8:30 a.m. Exercise

9:30 a.m. Study: say, InstantCert flashcards and a textbook.

12:30 p.m. Lunch

1:30 p.m. Study: say, a video lecture and more flashcards.

3:30 p.m. Break: run errands, go outside.

5:30 p.m. Homework: create and review notes.

6:30 p.m. Dinner

8:00 p.m. TV or a craft project

9:00 p.m. Read

10:00 p.m. Bedtime

Q: Hillary, how many subjects did you study at a time?

A: Just enough to keep it interesting. I found I was more motivated by completing a subject promptly and taking its corresponding test than by studying multiple subjects for the whole school year and taking all the corresponding tests at once. I usually budgeted three to six months for one or two long-term subjects, while allotting one or two months for short-term goals.

As an example, I studied Spanish throughout my junior year. In the meantime, I studied for the CompTIA A+ certification September-December, while I also prepared to take calculus in March. After I finished the A+ study, I began microeconomics, which I took in April.

There is no ideal course load that I know of, so don't hesitate to try studying a different number of subjects to find the quantity that keeps you learning, motivated, and on track to graduate.

FAQS FOR CHAPTER 8: WHERE TO GO FOR HELP

Q: I'm nervous that I'm going to get stuck on a hard problem while I'm studying and not be able to progress, and there won't be anyone to explain it to me. What do I do if this happens?

A: I got into this situation during my off-campus experience, and two instances are especially vivid. One was when I studied for DSST's Principles of Physical Science, and I was using a book of practice tests that included answers but no explanations of those answers. After using Dr. Jay L. Wile's science textbooks, I had become spoiled by his step-by-step explanations of complex subjects, which were only introduced once the student was prepped. The practice test book had no such explanations or sequencing. Sometimes the questions were so detailed that my high school textbooks didn't specifically address them, so I began researching the book's questions and answers by searching online. Through doing this I not only learned more about physical science, I corrected errors in the practice tests!

The other instance was during my study of calculus. The textbook I was using had some but not all answers in the back, and I didn't have the teacher's answer guide. There were a few problems that I just didn't understand no matter how much I reviewed or recalculated. In these cases, I turned to the internet again, tried to rephrase my problem in general terms, and scoured the search results. Sometimes this was laborious. But, I *did* find answers. There was one problem I left without hope of ever solving, only to discover further on in the textbook that I now had the skill to understand the earlier problem. That was a happy day.

So, for me, two sources helped me get past these roadblocks: the internet and my family. The internet showed me new ways to look at things, and my family let me work through problems with them, even if they didn't know the answer: many times saying the problem out loud elucidated the answer.

Other ideas for getting past these rough spots include tutoring and enrolling in a local class.

FAQS FOR CHAPTERS 9: ACCREDITATION

Q: What does accreditation mean?

A: Dictionary.com says *accredit* means "to certify (a school, college, or the like) as meeting all formal official requirements of academic excellence, curriculum, facilities, etc."[147]

Q: How do ACE and NCCRS credit recommendations compare to regional/national accreditation?

A: The American Council on Education (ACE) and the National College Credit Recommendation Service (NCCRS) are organizations that review college courses and give an estimate of how much *credit* the course is equivalent to. Regional and national accreditors, on the other hand, review institutions and programs to validate the *quality* of those institutions and programs. Thus, ACE and NCCRS have a different mission and purpose than do regional/national accreditors.

Q: What are degree mills and diploma mills?

A: A degree or diploma mill is a company or school that sells college diplomas that require little or no learning to earn. These companies are typically unaccredited or may be "accredited" through a counterfeit accreditor. Illegitimate accreditors sometimes have names similar to the six regional accreditors, which can be confusing. However, if you are able to pay a fee and walk away with a degree without any study or prior learning experience, this is a sure sign that the school is a mill. For more information, the following fact sheet published by the Council for Higher Education Accreditation (CHEA) lists some qualities of diploma mills and accreditation mills: http://chea.org/pdf/fact_sheet_6_diploma_mills.pdf.

Q: What is the difference between applying and enrolling at a college?

A: Applying to a college is the process of demonstrating that you meet their admission requirements. Once you fulfill these, the college will admit you. Some students will apply to more than one school at the same time to see which will accept them, or to receive an evaluation of the credits they have already earned.

After admission, enrollment is the next step. A student is enrolled at a school by paying tuition and/or registering for classes.

Q: I just received my evaluation, and I don't agree with how some of my credit transferred (some credit is worth less than at the credit-granting institution, the course code shows a different subject, etc.). Can I appeal this evaluation?

A: Yes. Before initiating the appeal process, inquire with your admissions counselor or advisor regarding the issue(s). Sometimes they will be able to correct your evaluation at your request. If they aren't able to help you, you can usually find out more about the appeal process on the college's website.

FAQS FOR CHAPTER 10: CHOOSING YOUR DEGREE, FINDING YOUR SCHOOL

Q: How should I compare schools offering degrees that are completed online?

A: Here are a few factors that can guide you when comparing several online degree programs.

- Accreditation: What type of accreditation does each college carry? Is the accreditation appropriate for your career field and goals regarding graduate education?

- Course content: Compare the degree plans. Does one school put more emphasis on certain areas of the degree? Will the courses prepare you for the type of work you will be pursuing?

- Price: Calculating the cost of similar online degrees at the different schools is one of the most enlightening ways to compare degrees. By roughing out a general plan of how you will complete the degree, including credit-by-exam testing and prior learning assessment, you can estimate your degree cost at each school.

- Time frame: If the school has many residency requirements, the degree could take longer to complete, due to being connected to the school's course structure and schedule. Conversely, if the school accepts many credit-by-exam tests, you will be able to create your own time frame for most of the degree and only be tied to the college structure for a short time.

- Transfer credit policy: How many credits can be transferred to the school? Does the school accept CLEP, DSST, and/or UExcel exams?

Q: How should I decide between the "Big Three?"

A: Each college has its own strengths and particular policies that will benefit select students. At DegreeForum.net, there are many threads devoted to determining the best school in general and the best school for a specific student. Many of the authors of these posts have valuable knowledge about one or more of the Big Three.

Here are two threads to get you started in discovering the minute differences between each school. You can also search the forum using keywords "Big Three comparison" for more information. Take note of the date of each thread, as you will need to update the given advice to match current college policy. (One significant example is TESU's change in 2014 to no longer accept FEMA courses for credit, raw or otherwise.)

- http://www.degreeforum.net/excelsior-thomas-edison-charter-oak-specific/18716-there-accepted-general-consensus-big-three.html (Initial post 03-25-2013)
- http://www.degreeforum.net/excelsior-thomas-edison-charter-oak-specific/18763-comparison-ec-vs-tesc-vs-cosc.html (Initial post 03-31-2013)
- http://www.degreeforum.net/excelsior-thomas-edison-charter-oak-specific/12199-updated-big-3-comparison.html (Initial post 10-13-2010)

Q: What separates the "Big Three" colleges of distance learning from other online colleges like the University of Phoenix?

A: The three main differences are:
1) The number of transfer credits accepted:
   - **Charter Oak State College**
     Community college credits: 87.[148]
     Transfer credit limit: No limit on total transfer credits stated on website.
   - **Excelsior College**
     Community college credits: 105.[149]
     Transfer credit limit: No limit on total transfer credits stated on website.
   - **Thomas Edison State University**
     Community college credits: 80.
     Transfer credit limit: 120 from a regionally accredited four-year institution (no limit on total transfer credits stated on website).[150]
   - **University of Phoenix**
     Community college credits: 54.[151]
     Transfer credit limit: 30 from national testing programs (including CLEP and DSST).[152]
2) The number of residency requirements:
   - **Charter Oak State College:** 6 credits—three-credit cornerstone course and three-credit capstone course.[153]

- **Excelsior College:** 3 credits—three-credit capstone course.[154]
- **Thomas Edison State University:** 4 credits—one-credit cornerstone course and three-credit capstone course (except the Bachelor of Arts in Business Administration, which does not require a capstone course).[155]
- **University of Phoenix:** At the time of printing, I was unable to find residency requirements listed on University of Phoenix's website; see transfer limits above.

3) The type of college:
- **Charter Oak State College:** Public.
- **Excelsior College:** Private nonprofit.
- **Thomas Edison State University:** Public.
- **University of Phoenix:** Private for-profit.

These are just a few of the criteria you can use to compare online schools. Other important factors are course quality, professor and faculty standards, tuition rates, accreditation, and the more intangible variables of college such as graduating in a state of well-being.[156]

Questions about Charter Oak State College:

Q: How can I satisfy the Information Literacy requirement?

A: There are several ways to satisfy the Information Literacy requirement, including passing Charter Oak State College's Information Literacy Test, which waives the course requirement. Some of the general education courses satisfy this course as well.

If you decide to complete the course, you can take it from Charter Oak or from another college and transfer it to Charter Oak. One popular, less expensive option is to take the course from Penn Foster College: the course costs $79 versus taking the course at Charter Oak which costs $287 for Connecticut residents/$377 for non-state residents during the 2016-2017 school year. For details, see http://www.charteroak.edu/Current/Academics/DegreeBasics/information-literacy-requirement.cfm and http://www.pennfoster.edu/college/all-programs/college-courses (click on "Information Literacy").

Questions about Thomas Edison State University

Q: What is the enrollment process like at Thomas Edison State University?

A: To begin the enrollment process, I paid the $75 application fee to Thomas Edison. Just over two weeks later, I received an email notifying me that I had been accepted and that in about four weeks I would receive a personalized evaluation using the transcripts I had sent to the university with my application. I received my evaluation within the stated time frame, and I was happy to find my credits had been applied very closely to my expectations.

Q: Is there any way I can estimate how my transferred courses will be accepted at TESU before I request an evaluation?

A: TESU's Prior Learning Assessment Course Description Database can be used to estimate how your credit will transfer. By searching the database for a course with a similar description to the course you have completed, you may get an idea what the course is worth at TESU. The database is available online: http://www2.tesu.edu/plasearch.php.

If you are in the military and have a Joint Services transcript, visit http://mvp.tesu.edu/ for a free evaluation of your military experience/credit *before you enroll!*

Q: Where can I find more information about earning an Associate in Science in Business Administration degree from TESU using open courses from Saylor.org?

A: Thomas Edison State University and Saylor.org have partnered to create a degree plan for an Associate in Science in Business Administration degree with degree requirements that can be fulfilled by completing free, online Saylor courses, CLEP tests, and portfolios at TESU. Because you must create portfolios to earn credit for completing the Saylor courses, this is not the least expensive associate degree, but it is certainly one option to be aware of.

Information about this program can be found on the following websites:
Saylor.org: https://learn.saylor.org/course/view.php?id=375.
TESU: http://www.tesu.edu/business/asba/Open-Course-Option.cfm.

FAQS FOR CHAPTER 11: HOW TO MAKE A DEGREE PLAN

Q: How do I start creating a degree plan?

A: The very first thing to do when creating a degree plan is to find the degree outline on the college's website. This outline is the bones of your degree plan, which you will flesh out in the next step. To find these degree plans, look for the degree requirements section or academic program information on the college's website. Colleges are required to make their program requirements available to the public, so even if you have to dig a little to find them, the degree outlines should be available somewhere on the college's website. From here you will be able to begin matching courses to the degree plan. *See* "Chapter 11: How to Make a Degree Plan."

Q: I'm looking for a credit-by-exam course equivalency chart from one of the Big Three colleges. Do you have direct links?

A: Yes, for COSC and TESU. Here they are:

- Charter Oak State College: http://www.charteroak.edu/exams/list-of-exams.cfm.
- Thomas Edison State University: http://www.tesu.edu/academics/catalog/index.cfm. (Equivalencies for TECEP tests begin on page 93, CLEP tests on page 100, and DSST tests on page 101 of the Undergraduate University Catalog.)
- In the past, Excelsior College has published a list of credit equivalencies in their Credit-by-Exam Catalog, but this catalog is currently unavailable. You might try searching their website for the catalog: http://www.excelsior.edu/static/search-result/?q=Credit-by-Exam%20Catalog.

FAQS FOR CHAPTER 12: SOCIALIZATION AND CREDENTIALING

Q: I am concerned that I will put myself at a disadvantage by not having the on-campus opportunities to discuss ideas and new concepts with my professor.

A: Rubbing minds with new people is a positive benefit of being on campus, but this doesn't always occur as often as we would hope, nor does being off-campus negate the opportunities to participate in discussions with mentors, college faculty, and other students. *Academically Adrift* mentions the following: "While 95 percent of college seniors in a large national sample reported having discussed 'grades or assignments' with an instructor, 29 percent reported that they had *never* discussed ideas from their readings or classes with faculty members outside of class during their last year in college. Intellectual engagement with faculty is even lower for younger students: 42 percent of first-year students have not discussed ideas from their readings or classes with faculty members outside of class."[157] *Academically Adrift* reports that the average student meets with faculty outside of class approximately once per month.[158] As an off-campus student, it would be very feasible to coordinate monthly meetings with an educational mentor, as well as exceed this limited mentor involvement.

Q: How does studying alone compare with studying with peers?

A: In *Academically Adrift*, this question is discussed using data gained from 2,322 students. These students took the Collegiate Learning Assessment (CLA) in their first semester as freshmen and again at the end of their sophomore year. Findings showed that the more time students spent studying alone, the more improvement they showed on the CLA test. The findings also showed that as students spent more time studying with peers, their improvement on the CLA test became smaller.[159]

Studying alone was a distinguishing student trait at schools where students improved the most on their CLA test. At these colleges and universities, students studied alone *almost three hours per week more* than students at other institutions. The authors note that three hours is quite significant, since their findings showed that students from all institutions on average studied alone less than nine hours per week.[160]

Q: What about fraternities and sororities?

A: *Academically Adrift* addresses this topic using the findings from their survey of 2,322 students. The authors discovered that the more time a student spent with a fraternity or sorority, the less improvement they showed on their Collegiate Learning Assessment (CLA) score. Even though students spending time in fraternities and sororities do "self-report higher levels of college satisfaction, campus involvement, and cognitive development," the authors state, "Measures of social integration thus either have no relationship or a negative relationship to learning. Different forms of social integration, including studying with peers and participating in fraternities and sororities, may have some positive consequences for integration and persistence; however, they are not the most appropriate mechanisms for fostering learning."[161]

Q: How will you find a spouse without going to college?

A: My sister and I gave an informational speech at a Mom's Meeting of our former homeschool group regarding college off campus, and this was one of the questions we were asked. Though the two of us and the moms chuckled together at this question, we all knew it was no laughing matter: many students attend college with the goal of meeting their spouse.

Our answer was that we would meet eligible men elsewhere. My sister and I certainly had opportunities during our college years to connect with others, including meeting people with shared hobbies or becoming acquainted with friends of friends. But what about other people? Do they have similar occasions to meet potential spouses, or are they really forfeiting a great opportunity by not going on campus?

In October 2013, Facebook released a compilation of findings regarding "a school's ability to introduce future spouses."[162] The data came from Facebook users who were at least 25 years old and who had attended the same high school or college as their spouse within four years of each other, implying that the school could have contributed to the meeting of the two people. The study found that about 28 percent of married college-graduates attended the same high school or college. The study did not discriminate *when* students met each other or if they became romantically involved before, during, or after high school/college, so the findings are "a rough proxy for the chance of finding a spouse at the school."

This same topic was studied in *Academically Adrift*'s follow-up research paper, which involved the students who were previously interviewed in *Academically Adrift* and who had now graduated within six years of entering college. Out of a total of 905 graduates, 153 graduates (17 percent) were married or cohabitating. Of those 153 married or cohabitating graduates, 42 percent had met their spouse or partner at college.[163]

Due to the qualitative nature of Facebook's study, and the small sample size of married or cohabitating graduates in *Academically Adrift*'s follow-up paper, neither 28 nor 42 percent is a definitive measure of the likelihood of finding a spouse at college. Still, this information is useful: if 90 percent of college graduates were finding their spouse at high school and college, then we would need to seriously consider the disadvantage off-campus students would have regarding meeting their spouse. By looking at the 72 percent of married college-graduates on Facebook who didn't attend the same college within four years of each other, and the 58 percent of married/cohabitating graduates who didn't become acquainted at college as found in *Academically Adrift*'s follow-up, it seems there are other effective ways to meet "the one," including being introduced online, through work, or by friends and family.

CLEP AND DSST TEST NOTES

MY CLEP TEST REVIEWS

In the style of the Specific Exam Feedback section on DegreeForum.net, I list my notes about the resources I used for ten of the CLEP tests I took. I created these notes after I took a test, and though I did not write an account for every test I took, these notes proved very beneficial for mapping out my next exam. It shocked me how quickly I forgot some of my favorite websites or study methods when I moved from one subject to the next. Because we each have unique learning styles and subject strengths, using these notes won't guarantee passing the test. However, they can be used as a starting platform to initiate your study.

For a comparison of CLEP exams in terms of difficulty, visit Free-Clep-Prep: http://www.free-clep-prep.com/clep-difficulty-list.html.

ANALYZING AND INTERPRETING LITERATURE	
Comments: I found out about this six-credit test through DegreeForum.net. I studied for one week, which gave me ample time to study. To prepare beyond the accumulation of reading comprehension skills learned in middle/high school, I took the practice test in the *CLEP Official Study Guide*, and briefly studied types of poems and their classification titles. While the ability to define and apply literary nouns and adjectives is needed to some extent, practical reading comprehension skills are the most important assets to have for this test.	Study Period: 1 week+
	Resources: • *CLEP Official Study Guide* • Reading comprehension study in middle/high school. • Online information about poems • Wikipedia

CALCULUS	
Comments: It was very helpful for me to gain a background in calculus by studying Larson and Hostetler's text, but REA's preparation book contains all the information needed to pass. However, if any of the ideas presented do not make sense or if you want to see them explained another way, other resources are needed. If I were to use an outdated textbook again (My Calculus was 2nd edition, copyright 1982), I would rigorously check that it is still relevant and motivating.	Study Period: 6½ months
	Resources: • *Calculus* by Larson and Hostetler • *CLEP Calculus (CLEP Test Preparation)* by REA

HUMAN GROWTH AND DEVELOPMENT

Comments: My prior preparation for CLEP Introductory Psychology provided a strong and surprisingly broad foundation for this test, my last CLEP (for now!) and the last needed for my degree. If I wanted a higher score, more study and completion of the listed materials would do the trick. InstantCert flashcards were good, but it was easy to get caught up in rote memory of the exact fill-in-the-blank term, rather than the holistic meaning and information in the flashcard. Reading the same information in book form was a great way to combat this. The REA's full-length tests with detailed answers are great!	Study Period: 4 weeks
	Resources: • InstantCert flashcards (went through all questions 1x, reviewing missed questions until all were correct) • Wikipedia • *Touch* by Tiffany Fields • REA Prep book (took Test #1 two days before test and scored a 69%) • *Life-Span Human Development* by Sigelman/Rider [7th edition, 2012] (read Introduction and one page of Ch. 1) • The Great Courses: "Theories of Human Development" taught by Professor Malcolm W. Watson (watched 7 of 24 lectures) • Free-Clep-Prep.com • DegreeForum.net (Very helpful, especially first-lady33's post)

INFORMATION SYSTEMS

Comments: My mom encouraged me to take this test to earn credit for the three-month study I did to prepare for the CompTIA A+ exam (since at that time TESU didn't give credit for any of the CompTIA exams). The textbooks I studied were *CompTIA A+ Cert Guide* and *CompTIA A+ Exam Cram*, referencing Wikipedia and additional websites for unfamiliar topics. Other than that preparation, I used the network section of the InstantCert flashcards to complete my study. Free-Clep-Prep.com has a substantial list of online articles and resources for this test. 　　The areas I felt weak in after taking the test were spreadsheet data terms and pseudocode, two terms included in the test's "Knowledge and Skills Required" outline (available online and in the *CLEP Official Study Guide*). More time with the InstantCert flashcards would probably have eliminated these study gaps. To gauge my preparedness, I used the practice test in the *CLEP Official Study Guide* and the sample questions available on CLEP's website.	Study Period: 3 months+
	Resources: 　• InstantCert.com 　• *CompTIA A+ Cert Guide* by Soper, Mueller, and Prowse 　• *CompTIA A+ Exam Cram* by David L. Prowse 　• *CLEP Official Study Guide* 　• Wikipedia

INTRODUCTORY PSYCHOLOGY

Comments: The test material is drawn from general knowledge of psychology and its basic terms. Using all of the listed resources helped me gain familiarity with the foreign concepts I needed to learn. *Introduction to Psychology and Counseling* covers almost everything presented on the test. The REA book encourages retention of information by bolding important facts and presenting information concisely. A brief physiological study of the brain would have been useful.	Study Period: 4 weeks+
	Resources: • *CLEP Official Study Guide* • *CLEP Introductory Psychology (CLEP Test Preparation)* by REA • *Introduction to Psychology and Counseling* by Meier, Minirth, Wichern and Ratcliff • InstantCert.com • http://psywww.com/selfquiz/ • http://allpsych.com/psychology101/

PRECALCULUS	
Comments: Using the Teaching Textbooks' *Pre-Calculus* text alone would have supplied the necessary information to pass this test. Be sure to download the 30-day trial of the test's graphing calculator (information available at http://clep.collegeboard.org/exam/precalculus). A solid understanding of trigonometry is needed to pass (Teaching Textbooks' *Pre-Calculus* is perfect for achieving this).	Study Period: 5 months
	Resources: • *Pre-Calculus: A Teaching Textbook* by Greg Sabouri and Shawn Sabouri • *Advanced Mathematics* by Saxon

PRINCIPLES OF MACROECONOMICS	
Comments: The InstantCert flashcards were very useful in preparing for this CLEP. Additional materials are only needed for variety or clarification of unfamiliar ideas. I also used the following resources: *CLEP Official Study Guide*: The practice questions are almost exactly like the test questions. The helpfulness of these questions alone nearly justifies the cost of the study guide! *Economics for Christian Schools*: Because of the book's age (copyright 1991), some of the information is outdated, but this book does provide many applicable graphs, charts, and tables. I used this to get a general overview and see economics through a Christian perspective. A basic economics textbook or reference book would provide a similar introduction to the subject. The Great Courses: "Economics": I have this series in DVD format, which gave me a break from reading and computer study. All the required topics for the CLEP test are presented; the hard part is gleaning those topics and committing them to memory. Regardless, it's a painless way to learn some economists' lingo and foundational concepts.	Study Period: 2 months
	Resources: • InstantCert flashcards • CLEP Official Study Guide • *Economics for Christian Schools* by Alan J. Carper • The Great Courses: "Economics" by Timothy Taylor

PRINCIPLES OF MICROECONOMICS

Comments: Common sense and reasoning go a long way in this test. Combine these with familiarity of economic terms and definitions, and you can pass this test. My prior study for macroeconomics laid the foundation for microeconomics, and I was glad I took micro after macro. The REA preparation book is not the most well-written of their series—too many ambiguous acronyms for the layman—but it covers the requisite points. The *CLEP Official Study Guide* is very accurate in judging readiness to test. The practice questions are extremely similar to the actual test.	Study Period: 3 weeks Resources: • *CLEP Official Study Guide* • *CLEP Microeconomics (CLEP Test Preparation)* by REA • The Great Courses: "Economics" by Timothy Taylor

SPANISH LANGUAGE

Comments: I took this test twice, earning a 52 (worth six credits) the first time and a 60 when I retested a year later. My goal in taking the test again was to earn a 63 for six additional credits at Thomas Edison State University. Even though I didn't reach that goal, my Spanish skills are better because of the additional year of study. Preparing for my first testing date included the knowledge I had gained through childhood Spanish lessons, Rosetta Stone Levels 1-4, REA's *CLEP Spanish Language* test prep, and general Spanish books. To improve my score 8 points, I spoke Spanish with a fluent Spanish-speaking friend twelve times over two months, used Rosetta Stone Level 5, read books in Spanish, used the *Berlitz Self-Teacher* book, studied verbs from *501 Spanish Verbs*, and took practice tests from REA's *CLEP Spanish Language* book. To do better on the test, I would need to immerse myself in speaking and reading the Spanish language.	Study Period: 4 years+ Resources: • Rosetta Stone Spanish Levels 1-5 • Childhood Spanish Lessons • Books in Spanish • *Berlitz Self-Teacher: Spanish* by Berlitz Editors • *501 Spanish Verbs* by Christopher Kendris and Theodore Kendris • Spanish-speaking friend • *CLEP Official Study Guide* • REA's *CLEP Spanish Language*

SOCIAL SCIENCES AND HISTORY	
Comments: The *CLEP Official Study Guide* in conjunction with *The Best Test Preparation for the CLEP* by REA gave an accurate preview of how the test turned out. *A Child's History of the World* is a good way to read about world history (it is the right depth of information). A solid background of American history is necessary. Study sociology if you haven't done so already. Learn about the main theories and their authors. See endnote 17 for a list of InstantCert's flashcard subjects you can use to prepare for this test.	Study Period: 5 months • Resources: • *CLEP Official Study Guide* • *The Best Test Preparation for the CLEP* by REA • *A Child's History of the World* by Virgil M. Hillyer

MY DSST TEST REVIEWS

Since I found others' test reviews on DegreeForum.net so informative and advisory, I wrote my own review after each DSST test I took. These notes helped me remember what resources I studied, how I put the information to memory, and where I could have improved my preparation. While each student's preferred study material will be slightly different, having a list of potential resources can help you find and choose those best for you.

Free-Clep-Prep compares the difficulty of the DSST exams here: http://www.free-clep-prep.com/dsst-difficulty-list.html.

A HISTORY OF THE VIETNAM WAR

Comments: The hardest part of this test was getting used to Vietnamese names. WGBH's American Experience series, "Vietnam: A Television History," helped tremendously with this, as I both <u>heard</u> names and places, and <u>saw</u> some of the key individuals I was studying. (This series would not be good for most youth under 15; it is war on film.) Once I got the main names cleared up, I was able to focus on the why and how. The questions on the test were straightforward. InstantCert did an excellent job preparing me. Once I started the test, I made a list on my scratch paper of the U.S. presidents in office during this period, which gave me a visual time frame I could reference and add to throughout the test.	Study Period: 4 weeks
	Resources: • InstantCert • DegreeForum.net • WGBH's "Vietnam: A Television History" (11 hrs.) • Timeline in *Vietnam: A History* by Stanley Karnow • Wikipedia Total study time: 29 hours

AN INTRODUCTION TO THE MODERN MIDDLE EAST

Comments: I scheduled this test after one month of study, but the day before testing I was so nervous that I almost canceled the test to study for another month. On the day before the exam, I scored a 71% on the 14 questions in DSST's Fact Sheet and 55% on the 100-question test from Free-Clep-Prep.com. The Free-Clep-Prep test was very helpful, not just because of the greater number of questions, but because it simulated the diverse and far-reaching nature of the actual test. InstantCert's flashcards were a superb foundation for study. I was glad to have Wikipedia to clarify and expand certain topics and biographies. Using Wikipedia also helped me retain more of the information in the flashcards.

During the test, I wrote from memory a list of Iranian leaders (shahs, prime ministers, and Khomeini) who were in power during the twentieth century. This was handy!

If I had to take the test again and I wanted to be less nervous, my study for the test would include writing out a list of rulers along with which country they led, when they led, and what significant changes they made. Creating this list would have helped me organize and internalize those facts in my mind. However, being as nervous as I was pushed me to study hard right before the test—and achieve a credit-earning score!

Study Period: 4 weeks

Resources:
- InstantCert flashcards (3x through, ≈16 hours, made notes)
- DegreeForum.net Exam Specific Feedback
- Wikipedia
- *The Modern Middle East: A History* by James L. Gelvin (read 1/3 of book; great resources in back: timeline, biographical sketches and glossary)
- Free-Clep-Prep.com's free practice test
- The Great Courses: "Great World Religions: Islam" (watched 4 of 12 lectures)
- The Great Courses: "United States and the Middle East: 1914 to 9/11" (listened to 4 of 24 lectures)
- *Israel: An Illustrated History* by Daniel J. Schroeter (read first two chapters)
- Snazzlefrag's study guide from Free-Clep-Prep.com
- Interactive Middle East map: http://lizardpoint.com/geography/mideast-quiz.php
- Middle East flashcards: http://quizlet.com/9442165/flashcards
- Saylor Academy's Modern Middle East and Southwest Asia course: http://www.saylor.org/courses/hist232/ (I didn't use this course, but it looks useful.)

MONEY AND BANKING	
Comments: This test was a very practical yet somewhat obscure test: all the more reason to learn the material as it affects us every day! Macroeconomics is heavily drawn upon, as is information about commercial banking, which wasn't as easy as I had hoped it would be! Not only do you need to know the facts, but you also need to apply what you know in what-would-happen-if questions. InstantCert's flashcards were very helpful, as was my own study on Keynesianism and monetarism. Knowing about fiscal and monetary policy and their different effects on the economy is mandatory. DegreeForum.net's Exam Specific Thread is very informative and includes user-submitted downloadable study guides.	Study Period: 4 weeks Resources: InstantCert • "Money & Banking DSST study guide IC Part 1" and "M&B_notes" (two study guides from DegreeForum.net's Exam Specific Thread) • *Economics Deciphered: A Layman's Survival Guide* by Maurice Levi • Past study of macroeconomics • Wikipedia Total study time: 16 hours

ORGANIZATIONAL BEHAVIOR

Comments: This was a very straightforward test. Many of the key theories I had learned in my study for CLEP Introductory Psychology (e.g. operant vs. classical conditioning) were reintroduced. This made my study easier because I needed only to review these theories and apply them to organizations (rather than learn them from scratch). InstantCert was excellent for this! Not only did the flashcards define the necessary terms, they gave many examples of these terms in a business scenario. Because I was studying two subjects at once (and this was the easier subject for me), I didn't go through the last three sets of flashcards but instead used the glossary and study guide listed in Resources. The practice test from FinishCollegeFast.com was helpful, as was the 100-question test at Free-Clep-Prep.com. Once again, the exam specific thread at DegreeForum.net was right on in pinpointing what and how deep to study.	Study Period: 4 weeks
	Resources: • InstantCert flashcards (studied for about 10 hours, made notes) • Degreeforum.net Exam Specific Thread • Previous study for CLEP Introductory Psychology • *Organizational Behavior* by Jennifer M. George & Gareth R. Jones, 3rd ed. (only read half of chapter 1, but textbook seems to be very thorough and explanatory with many real-life examples.) • Glossary from *Organizational Behavior: Solutions for Management* by Sweeney and McFarlin online at http://highered.mheducation.com/sites/0073659088/student_view0/glossary.html • Study guide on the Exam Specific Thread created by rmroberts (post #52) • Practice test from FinishCollegeFast.com

PERSONAL FINANCE

Comments: The scoring range for this test is 200-500, and 400 is the passing score.[164] I earned 394, making Personal Finance the first credit-by-exam test I failed. I was so disappointed and angry with myself! I feel I didn't study deeply enough and in the right areas until a week before the test. The last two resources listed were the most helpful; I just didn't absorb enough of their information. If I made a recommendation to myself, I would buy a book specifically about personal finance and use InstantCert heavily.	Study Period: 1 month
	Resources: • *Economics for Christian Schools* by Alan J. Carper (read about half; helpful; could have read whole book for broad overview) • *The World's Easiest Pocket Guide to Buying Your First House* • *The World's Easiest Pocket Guide to Buying Insurance* (reading even more about insurance would have been advantageous) • InstantCert (used for two days before testing; questions were right on)

PRINCIPLES OF PHYSICAL SCIENCE I

Comments: I used (and corrected!) *Rudman's Questions and Answers on the DSST in Physical Science*. This text has about 24 tests that, when combined with internet study (Wikipedia and science sites), broadened my knowledge. Beware—this study guide can be extremely frustrating because many of the test answers are incorrect. I also used Dr. Wile's *Exploring Creation with Chemistry* and *Exploring Creation with Physics*. It would have been good for me to specifically review acceleration due to gravity.	Study Period: 7 months+
	Resources: • Wikipedia • *Exploring Creation with Chemistry* by Jay L. Wile • *Exploring Creation with Physics* by Jay L. Wile • *Rudman's Questions and Answers on the DSST in Physical Science* • Science-related websites

HISTORY OF THE SOVIET UNION

Comments: I memorized a list of rulers and dates which I wrote on my scratch paper after the test started. The questions on this test were worded for more specific and detailed answers, befitting for an upper-level course. InstantCert pulled through again, laying an excellent foundation for my study. Wikipedia and DegreeForum.net filled in and clarified any vague flashcards. I used these three plus a few online resources to pass this test with a 59 (score needed to pass: 45 of a possible 80). There are at least two free practice tests: one specifically for the DSST test at Free-Clep-Prep.com and the other covering European history between 1919 and 1938 at sparknotes.com (look for the review test for The Interwar Years [1919-1938] in the history section). I didn't use either practice test because I only learned about them a few days before my test. Note to self: Check the Exam Specific thread more than once during study, and don't wait until two days before you test to read the thread!	Study Period: 4 weeks Resources: • Wikipedia • InstantCert flashcards • Degreeforum.net • www.studenthandouts.com/01-Web-Pages/001-Pages/10.20.Collapse-Soviet-Union-OUTLINE.htm (simple outline of Soviet Union history found through a Google search) • Notes by DegreeForum.net user jwill340@gmail.com on the Exam Specific thread (Very helpful!) Total study time: 28 hours

SUBSTANCE ABUSE	
Comments: InstantCert flashcards were my primary resource. I went through all the cards twice, the first time repeating the flashcards answered incorrectly until all were correct. The flashcards were excellent preparation for this straightforward test. For variety, I used a few online websites to supplement the flashcards.	Study Period: 3 weeks
	Resources: • InstantCert flashcards • http://www.drugfree.org/drug-guide/ (descriptions of drugs with pictures, which helped me differentiate the requisite drugs) • *Drugs, Society & Human Behavior* Online Learning Center from McGraw-Hill: http://highered.mheducation.com/sites/0073380903/student_view0/chapter1/index.html (I played a concentration game which is no longer available; current resources include quizzes and flashcards.) • Free-Clep-Prep.com has a selection of free, online resources.

THE CIVIL WAR AND RECONSTRUCTION

Comments: This test was definitely clear-cut and worded like a 200-level test (think DSST's A History of the Vietnam War). There are so many study resources! Instant-Cert served me very well, and SparkNotes helped cement dates into my mind. Degree-Forum.net's Exam Specific Thread precisely describes this test.

I made fact sheets for generals, unfamiliar terms and each year of the war. This rehearsal of much of the same information I had typed into my personal notes from the InstantCert flashcards proved to be an important step for internalizing what I was learning.

DegreeForum.net user RangerAV8R shared the following handy mnemonic for memorizing the order of secession: **S**outhern **M**en **F**ought **A**gainst **G**rant & **L**incoln **T**o **V**indicate **A** **T**roubled **N**ation (South Carolina, Mississippi, Florida, Alabama, Georgia, Louisiana, Texas, Virginia, Arkansas, Tennessee, North Carolina).

User happy23211 mentioned the following mnemonic, **F**our **B**ulls **A**te **E**verything **V**icky **G**rew, for the timeline of major Civil War events: Fort Sumter, Bull Run, Antietam, Emancipation Proclamation, Vicksburg, and Gettysburg.

Study Period: 4 weeks

Resources:
- InstantCert (once through flashcards re-doing missed questions until all were correct, spent approx. 17 hrs)
- Wikipedia
- Free-Clep-Prep.com
- Finishcollegefast.com (for free 10-question pretest)
- Degreeforum.net (Exam Specific Thread is REALLY, REALLY HELPFUL!)
- SparkNotes: The Civil War (online study guide and quiz)
- DSST Fact Sheet (the 12 sample questions were slightly easier than the actual test)

WESTERN EUROPE SINCE 1945

Comments: InstantCert flashcards prepared me so well for this test! The test questions were focused more on events and their causes, rather than rote memorization of dates. However, all the dates I did memorize helped me keep countries, wars, and rulers, from getting mixed up. The posts on the Specific Exam Feedback section of DegreeForum.net were very accurate. I probably could have passed solely studying the flashcards, as all the necessary information was there, but the other resources opened my eyes to the facts I had not memorized or noticed. Making a physical timeline, taking flashcard notes, and writing out major countries' leaders and government structures worked well for me.	Study Period: 5 weeks
	Resources: • InstantCert • *The Story of the World: History for the Classical Child, Vol. 4* by Susan Wise Bauer • Wikipedia • Europa.eu • Charts of Britain, France, Spain, Italy, Germany, and the EU's structures created by DegreeForum.net user daniellevine and downloaded from DegreeForum.net Total study time: 17 hours

GLOSSARY

ACE	(American Council on Education) A consortium of accredited, degree-granting colleges and universities. One of their functions is to review coursework completed through apprenticeships, training programs, certifications and examinations, and then provide credit recommendations for colleges to use when awarding credit.
ALEKS	(Assessment and LEarning in Knowledge Spaces) An online tutoring-style company that offers courses between kindergarten and college level. ALEKS courses are adaptive to your learning level and help you hone in on the areas of a subject that are unfamiliar. As of March 2016, nine ALEKS courses have been recommended by the ACE for college credit. ALEKS are accepted by the "Big Three."

B&M	Brick and mortar, usually referring to classes taken on campus or the on-campus portion of college.
THE "BIG THREE"	While this generally means Harvard, Yale, and Princeton, in the world of distance learning the "Big Three" are Charter Oak State College, Excelsior College, and Thomas Edison State University. The trio has earned this nickname because they are the top three colleges in America for accepting transferred credit. Credit accepted by these three can be earned from community colleges, other colleges or universities, credit-by-exam tests, prior learning assessment, and certifications. Each of the "Big Three" is regionally accredited.
CLEP	(College Level Examination Program) A testing program owned by the College Board (the maker of the SAT) that is used for earning college credit in 33 subjects. These tests are accepted at over 2,900 colleges and universities.
COSC	(Charter Oak State College) An online public college in New Britain, Connecticut. The college is accredited by the New England Association of Schools and Colleges and by the Connecticut Board of Governors for Higher Education.
CREDIT-BY-EXAM TEST	A test developed to allow students to show their level of knowledge in a particular subject. Analogous to "testing out" of a class.
DANTES	(Defense Activity for Non-Traditional Education Support) DANTES supports the off-duty voluntary education programs of the Department of Defense and offers educational opportunities and assistance to service members and veterans. DANTES provides the popular credit-by-exam DSST tests which are available to service members, veterans, and civilians alike.
DEGREEFORUM.NET	Online discussion forum owned by InstantCert.com. Most of the forum is open for anyone to view and post.

DEGREEFORUM.WIKIA.COM	A collaborative website in the style of Wikipedia dedicated to helping people earn their degree through credit-by-exam testing and credit transfer. Here you can find actual degree plans used by graduates of the "Big Three." You can also find answers to common questions related to earning a degree off campus.
DISTANCE LEARNING	A broad term covering learning completed at a distance from the college. Includes online classes, correspondence courses, and credit-by-exam tests.
DSST	A credit-by-exam test designed for the military but available for civilians as well. Computer based and offered at Prometric testing locations and at military bases; 34 exam titles.
EC	(Excelsior College) Private nonprofit institution in Albany, New York founded in 1971. Philosophy: What you know is more important than where or how you learned it.®
ECE	(Excelsior College Examinations) Outdated acronym for Excelsior College's own brand of credit-by-exam tests. Now called UExcel.
ETS	(Educational Testing Service) A nonprofit organization that owns the testing company Prometric and develops and administers tests including CLEP and GRE.
FCC	(Frederick Community College) A community college in Frederick, Maryland. This college name turns up frequently on DegreeForum.net, as students will send transcripts from FEMA and other programs to FCC to earn college credit, which can then be transferred to other colleges. The reason for this intermediate step is that some colleges do not accept FEMA and other program transcripts "raw," but they will accept them as courses earned through FCC.

FEMA	(Federal Emergency Management Agency) An agency of the United States Department of Homeland Security. FEMA pertains to off-campus learning through their Emergency Management Courses. These online-based courses are freely available and can be submitted to certain colleges for credit.
GED	A high school diploma equivalency program. The GED test contains four subjects: reasoning through language arts, mathematical reasoning, science, and social studies. The four subjects can be completed one subject at a time in the order you choose.
GRE	A graduate admissions test covering verbal reasoning, quantitative reasoning, and analytical writing.
GMAT	A graduate business admissions exam. The test measures analytical writing, integrated reasoning, and quantitative and verbal skills.
INSTANTCERT	Online website offering study flashcards for CLEP, DSST, UExcel, and TECEP tests.
MOOC	(Massive Open Online Course) A college-level course made available to the public (usually via the Internet) designed to promote high-quality, low-to-no cost learning for students of all ages.
ONLINE COLLEGE CLASS	A college course that has been created or modified to be completed online. Some courses are available entirely online, whereas other courses use a textbook and other offline material with the tests online. Usually these courses will have a professor available to answer questions and grade assignments and tests.
PROMETRIC	Test administration company that administers DSST exams among other tests.

STRAIGHTERLINE	A company offering classes at the college level with ACE credit recommendations. These classes are not as widely accepted as CLEP or DSST tests, but the "Big Three" accept most, if not all, of StraighterLine's courses.
TECEP	(Thomas Edison Credit by Exam Program) Credit-by-exam tests that are developed and offered by Thomas Edison State University.
TESC	*See* TESU.
TESU	(Thomas Edison State University, formerly Thomas Edison State College) Four-year public university in Trenton, New Jersey established in 1972. Specifically designed for adults who want to go back to school and those who wish to earn their degree off campus. Students under 21 are accepted on a case-by-case basis.
UEXCEL	Credit-by-exam tests created by Excelsior College. Previously called ECE.

BIBLIOGRAPHY

Arum, Richard, and Josipa Roksa. *Academically Adrift*. Chicago: The University of Chicago Press, 2011.

Bok, Derek. *Universities in the Marketplace: The Commercialization of Higher Education*. Princeton: Princeton University Press, 2003.

Bowen, William G. *Higher Education in the Digital Age*. Princeton: Princeton University Press, 2013.

Bower, Beverly L. and Kimberly P. Hardy, eds. *From Distance Education to E-Learning: Lessons Along the Way*. San Francisco: Wiley Periodicals, Inc., 2004.

Cook-DeRosa, Jennifer. *Homeschooling for College Credit*. San Bernardino, 2012.

Khan, Salman. *The One World Schoolhouse*. New York: Twelve, 2012.

Nathan, Rebekah. *My Freshman Year: What a Professor Learned By Becoming a Student.* Ithaca: Cornell University Press, 2005.

Selingo, Jeffrey J. *College (Un)Bound.* Boston: Houghton Mifflin Harcourt, 2013.

Voeller, Brad. *Accelerated Distance Learning.* Hinsdale: Dedicated Publishing, 2002.

ACKNOWLEDGEMENTS

In compiling and researching the nuances of off-campus college learning, I found encouragement and support from the following people. They enabled me to bring my findings to a wider audience.

DegreeForum members made my college journey smoother by sharing their experiences through their generous forum posts. Their research, sometimes to the depths of college websites to find obscure but consequential information regarding degree plans and test preparation, gave me a springboard for launching my own study.

I am grateful to Brad Voeller for his enthusiasm when I approached him with my completed manuscript and for taking time to review my work. His own book changed my life.

My deep appreciation goes to Stewart A. Williams for the interior formatting. His design not only brought the book to life but also enhanced its readability.

Having Laura Shelley involved to create such a comprehensive index was a pleasure. She was both conscientious and considerate.

Micah Kandros lightened my book task with his creation of cover designs to represent the book's key concepts. Through each design round, his cheerful emails kept the project moving forward with ease.

To help me weed my words, Nancy Halseide provided a thorough and kind edit of my manuscript and offered many improvements for clarity and succinctness.

To my friends and family I send the warmest thanks for the inquiries of how the book was progressing, the conversations on the topic of higher education, and the time spent brainstorming titles and selecting the final cover design.

Roberta Windham provided me with invaluable feedback, as both she and her family had watched me complete my degree and could compare what they saw with what I wrote. Roberta's astute thoughts on both the content and execution of the book helped me bring it to final form. Thank you, Roberta, for sharing *Accelerated Distance Learning* with my family!

My four grandparents, Bill & Judy and LaMar & Vicky, each contributed to this book with their time, life stories, and words of encouragement. I give them my unending thanks.

Lauren Anne went the extra mile with my book project, brightening my sequestered writing space with visits to check on how I was doing or bring me hot cocoa. The insights she furnished from her own college experience added depth to my narrative.

I am grateful for the discussions with my dad in which he helped me unpack and understand the social connections that we as a society equate with the college experience. He encouraged me to take thoughtful risks, including tackling and completing a project that was in a vein removed from what I had pursued in life so far.

I wish to thank my mom, who gave me the idea that I might one day write a book about earning credit off campus. She provided a listening ear for me to sound my concerns, frustrations, and successes, as well as tirelessly read and edited each draft of my manuscript.

ENDNOTES

¹ *average price of $14,262 per year* The figure of $14,262 was the average cost, including in-state tuition, fees, room, and board, of the 2008-2009 school year for a full-time student at a public, 4-year institution. The same year at a private nonprofit 4-year institution cost an average of $33,804. For the 2013-2014 school year, these costs had risen to $18,110 and $40,708, respectively. Digest of Education Statistics (2014), "Table 330.10. Average undergraduate tuition and fees and room and board rates charged for full-time students in degree-granting postsecondary institutions, by level and control of institution: 1963-64 through 2013-14," U.S. Department of Education, Institute of Education Sciences, National Center for Education Statistics. http://nces.ed.gov/programs/digest/d14/tables/dt14_330.10.asp.

² *working full time earned an average of $30,000 per year* Digest of Education Statistics (2014), "Table 502.30. Median annual earnings of full-time year-round workers 25 to 34 years old and full-time year-round workers as a percentage of the labor force, by sex, race/ethnicity, and educational attainment: Selected years, 1995 through 2013," U.S. Department of Education, Institute of Education Sciences, National Center for Education Statistics. http://nces.ed.gov/programs/digest/d14/tables/dt14_502.30.asp.

³ *those with a bachelor's degree earned on average $20,000 more* High school graduates and GED holders had the median earnings of $30,731 while those with a bachelor's degree had the median earnings of $51,308. Annual Social and Economic Supplement (2014), "Table PINC-03. Educational Attainment--People 25 Years Old

and Over, by Total Money Earnings in 2014, Work Experience in 2014, Age, Race, Hispanic Origin, and Sex," U.S. Census Bureau. http://www.census.gov/hhes/www/cpstables/032015/perinc/pinc03_000.htm.

[4] **39 percent higher** The average total tuition, fees, room and board rates (in constant 2012-2013 dollars) charged for full-time undergraduate students at public institutions was $10,800 in 2002-2003 and $15,022 in 2012-2013. Digest of Education Statistics (2013), "Fast Facts: Tuition costs of colleges and universities," U.S. Department of Education, Institute of Education Sciences, National Center for Education Statistics, accessed April 7, 2016. http://nces.ed.gov/fastfacts/display.asp?id=76.

[5] **the amount of time spent working to pay off debt** The National Survey of Student Engagement found "that about 32 percent of freshman and 36 percent of seniors reported that financial concerns had interfered with their academic performance; this proportion rose to almost 60 percent for full-time seniors who worked twenty-one or more hours per week." National Survey of Student Engagement, *Promoting Student Learning and Institutional Improvement: Lessons from NSSE at 13: Annual Results 2012* (Bloomington: Indiana University of Postsecondary Research, 2012), 17, as quoted in William G. Bowen, *Higher Education in the Digital Age* (Princeton: Princeton University Press, 2013.), 38, note 61.

[6] **That's a commute!** Two examples of students who took an airplane to a testing center are DegreeForum.net users Irnbru from Scotland, and OE800_85 who flew from Shanghai to Manila, Philippines. Although DSSTs are offered around the world at various locations, not all countries have a testing center. Sometimes international students come to the U.S. to take their tests for more flexibility in testing office hours and less wait time. As of April 2016, the DSST website lists 100 international testing locations. http://getcollegecredit.com/institutions/search.

[7] **average room and board paid by full-time college students** Trends in Higher Education, "Tuition and Fees and Room and Board over Time, Table 2: Average Tuition and Fees and Room and Board (Enrollment-Weighted) in Current Dollars and in 2015 Dollars, 1971-72 to 2015-16," The College Board, accessed April 7, 2016. http://trends.collegeboard.org/college-pricing/figures-tables/tuition-and-fees-and-room-and-board-over-time-1.

[8] **Postponing enrollment saved me over $7,500.** Thomas Edison State University's Enrolled Options Plan ($2,445/yr for out-of-state residents) plus the Technology Services Fee ($100/yr) for three years equal $7,635 (using 2008-09 tuition rates). Actual costs would have been more due to increasing tuition. Tuition rate from *Colleges in the Middle Atlantic States*, 25th ed. (Lawrenceville: Peterson's, 2009), 67.

[9] **as many as nine credits** College of Central Florida: nine credits awarded. *2015-2016 College Catalog*, 39. http://www.cf.edu/Assets/files/catalogs/2015_2016_catalog.pdf.

[10] **financial aid can prove to be less helpful than it appears** The author of *Homeschooling for College Credit*, Jennifer Cook-DeRosa, explains the scholarship dilemma succinctly in a DegreeForum.net post about Pell Grants, a grant which can be used by enrolled students both on campus and off campus, with up to $5,815 for

the 2016-17 school year (rates change yearly) available per student. At TESU, a Pell Grant has to be used for a minimum of six credits per term over four terms. She writes to a mom searching for scholarship money for her son, "You can still see if he qualifies for a Pell Grant ($5600 gift) but that will have to be used by taking 6 credits per term x 4 terms. The cost to USE THAT MONEY is $8940, for a net due of $3340.... so not really a savings and you still have to raise $3340 plus books." cookderosa, September 29, 2012, comment on thread, "Scholarships or Grants?," DegreeForum. net, September 29, 2012. http://www.degreeforum.net/general-education-testing-discussion/17503-scholarships-grants.html#post133283.

[11] **Each offers an array of scholarships** Thomas Edison State University Scholarships: http://www.tesu.edu/tuition/Scholarships.cfm.
Excelsior College Scholarships: http://www.excelsior.edu/scholarships.
Charter Oak State College Financial Aid Programs: http://www.charteroak.edu/current/sfa/types.cfm.

[12] **"By my math, that's a $36,000 scholarship!"** cookderosa, September 29, 2012, comment on thread, "Scholarships or Grants?," DegreeForum.net, September 29, 2012. http://www.degreeforum.net/general-education-testing-discussion/17503-scholarships-grants.html#post133283.

[13] **the Lifetime Learning Credit and the American Opportunity Credit** Lifetime Learning Credit on the IRS website: http://www.irs.gov/publications/p970/ch03. html.
American Opportunity Credit on the IRS website: http://www.irs.gov/publications/p970/ch02.html.

[14] **a $1900 down payment with a $195 monthly subscription Unbound:** https://collegeplus.org/unbound.
Pathway: https://collegeplus.org/pathway.
Prep: https://collegeplus.org/prep. Accessed April 6, 2016.

[15] **CLEP banks your test scores** "What Your Score Means" PDF document: http://clep.collegeboard.org/about/score. Accessed April 6, 2016.

[16] **Two places to begin the search** DegreeForum.net: http://www.degreeforum.net/ and Degree Forum Wiki: http://degreeforum.wikia.com/.

[17] **a company offering study information covering 25 of the current 33 CLEP tests** The CLEP exams not covered by InstantCert include French, German, Spanish, Calculus, Chemistry, Natural Sciences, College Composition Modular, and Social Sciences & History.
However, InstantCert's Biology flashcards can be used to study for the Natural Sciences Test; the College Composition flashcards will help with College Composition Modular (especially since these two tests assess the same set of skills in a slightly different format); and the flashcards covering United States History I and II, Western Civilization I and II, American Government, Introductory Sociology, Introductory Psychology, Macroeconomics, and Microeconomics may assist in preparing for the Social Sciences and History test.

The following websites can be used to compare CLEP test titles with the study resources offered by InstantCert: http://clep.collegeboard.org/exam and http://www.instantcert.com/college.php4?tab=subjects. Accessed April 6, 2016.

[18] *use a search engine with the keywords "McGraw Hill"* An example of McGraw-Hill's supplemental resources is those for the Spanish language textbook *Puntos de Partida*, which can be found here: http://highered.mheducation.com/sites/0072873949/student_view0/index.html. Be sure to use the drop-down box on the left to view the resources for each chapter. Accessed April 6, 2016.

[19] *the form available on the College Board website* CLEP transcript form: http://clep.collegeboard.org/about/score.

[20] *I can expect to pay $10,984* Cost of Attendance - Undergraduate Students, WSU Pullman Campus (In-State), Estimates for Fall 2016 - Spring 2017: http://finaid.wsu.edu/cost-of-attendance/. Accessed April 1, 2016.

[21] *each lower-division credit costs $410 plus approximately $15 in fees* According to the Tuition and Fees Calculator on www.phoenix.edu, tuition as of April 2016 is $410 per lower-division credit, and there is a materials and fees charge of $1,120 for 24 courses. This charge "covers the cost of electronic course materials, books and any fees throughout your program." The charge per course is $46.67 ($1,120 divided by 24). Because I excluded materials and books in this comparison of per-credit costs, I arbitrarily divided $46.67 by three to approximate the fees alone at $15.56 per credit.

[22] *The CLEP per-credit cost is as follows* For these figures, I assumed that 50% of the bachelor's degree was earned using CLEP (though the figures would be nearly identical if a similarly-priced credit-by-exam test such as DSST was substituted), and the other 50% was earned through online courses from the three colleges, respectively, as an out-of-state student. The reason I designated how the rest of the degree was earned beyond CLEP tests is that how you earn those credits determines which tuition plan you choose. I only included enrollment costs for two years to cover the online courses, since CLEP tests can be earned without being enrolled. The final per-credit number is unweighted between the CLEP tests and online courses.
The CLEP tests are assumed as follows: four 6-credit tests plus twelve 3-credit tests for a total of 60 credits. The total number of CLEP tests pertinent to a specific degree varies; I used CLEP to fulfill 58% of my bachelor's degree in social sciences. Note that while the college courses have a set time frame with an enrollment period (two years in this example) and scheduled semesters during which the courses can be taken, the CLEP tests have no set time frame. You could earn them in 6 months or 6 years! Your credit will be applicable to a degree anytime in the 20 years that CLEP holds each score.
The following figures reflect the 2016-2017 school year rates.
Charter Oak: $24,862 for 60 credits over 2 years plus $1,760 for 16 CLEP tests equals $26,622.
Excelsior: $31,195 for 60 credits over 2 years plus $1,760 for 16 CLEP tests equals $32,955.
Thomas Edison: $19,102 for 60 credits over 2 years plus $1,760 for 16 CLEP tests equals $20,862.

References: Charter Oak State College Net Cost Calculator: http://www.charteroak.edu/prospective/tuition/.
Excelsior College Tuition Estimator: http://www.excelsior.edu/costs-and-financing.
Thomas Edison State University Cost Calculator: http://www.tesu.edu/tuition/how-much.cfm.

[23] *members of the following are eligible* See CLEP's military page for the DANTES Eligibility Chart: http://clep.collegeboard.org/military.

[24] *submit an application for reimbursement* Per http://www.benefits.va.gov/gibill/national_testing.asp and http://clep.collegeboard.org/military/veterans.

[25] *your first attempt of each DSST title is funded* For more information, see the DANTES Funding Guide PDF and the military section on the DSST Test Takers webpage: http://getcollegecredit.com/test_takers/.

[26] *list of accepted DSST tests and their corresponding course numbers* Here are two example lists of DSST tests shown with their school-specific course numbers:
University of Northwestern - St Paul: https://www.unwsp.edu/web/registrar/credit-by-examination.
Thomas Edison State University: http://www.tesu.edu/current-students/Publications.cfm, University Catalog (PDF version), page 101. Accessed April 1, 2016.

[27] *keywords "McGraw Hill HigherEd" and the name of your test subject* The following resource page for the textbook *Organizational Behavior* is an example of McGraw-Hill's supplements. I found the glossary especially informative. http://highered.mheducation.com/sites/0073659088/student_view0/index.html.

[28] *a recommendation as to how many college credits each is worth.* http://www.acenet.edu/higher-education/topics/Pages/Credit-Evaluations.aspx.

[29] *visit ACE's website to view their catalog of courses* http://www2.acenet.edu/credit/.

[30] *approximately 5,200 courses and educational programs* http://www.nationalccrs.org/about/history.
courses can be found in the College Credit Recommendations Directory. http://www.nationalccrs.org/ccr/home.html.

[31] *navigate to the area of their website that deals with transferring credit* "Earn More Credit Through Prior Learning & Experience," Liberty University, http://www.liberty.edu/online/credit-for-prior-learning/.

[32] *transferring your ALEKS course to your ACE transcript* https://www2.acenet.edu/credit?fuseaction=transcripts.main.

[33] *the limit of credits that can be transferred from accredited community colleges* The credit limits are sourced from the following websites:
Charter Oak State College: http://www.charteroak.edu/prospective/new/faq.

cfm#18; see also http://www.charteroak.edu/community-college/.
Excelsior College: http://www.excelsior.edu/web/partners/community-colleges.
Thomas Edison State University: http://www.tesu.edu/admissions/Transfer-Credit.
cfm.

[34] *none of FEMA's Independent Study courses have ACE credit recommendations* The
on-campus credit-recommendations can be viewed by selecting National Emergency
Training Center (EMI) from ACE's list of organizations (direct link: http://www2.
acenet.edu/credit/?fuseaction=browse.getOrganizationDetail&FICE=300757). If
any Independent Study courses had credit recommendations, they would be listed
here and could be identified by their course letter prefix, IS (e.g. IS-230.d)

[35] *Frederick Community College, which has a dedicated program for FEMA credit
transfer.* Frederick Community College's website is http://www.frederick.edu/, and
their EM-Study (Emergency Management Study) site is http://em-study.com/.

[36] *FEMA credits are no longer accepted at TESU* Per http://www.tesu.edu/military/
army/Credit-Banking.cfm.

[37] *other tests available from ACTFL that assess skills other than speaking.* Other
tests offered by the American Council on the Teaching of Foreign Languages assess
speaking, reading & listening, and writing. http://www.actfl.org/professional-
development/proficiency-assessments-the-actfl-testing-office.
For the Oral Proficiency Interview by Computer (OPIc), there is a demo available that
gives you an opportunity to become familiar with the program. Using the demo in
your target language might be a good way to practice for the phone interview version
of the OPI as well as the computer-based version. http://www.languagetesting.com/
oral-proficiency-interview-by-computer-opic.

[38] *ACE recommends: up to 6 lower-level and 6 upper-level* Credit recommendation
for course/exam title "ACTFL Oral Proficiency Interview (OPI): Advanced High/
Superior." http://www2.acenet.edu/credit/?fuseaction=browse.getOrganizationDet
ail&FICE=300017. Accessed March 31, 2016.

[39] *ACE recommends: 3-16 lower-level* Select an exam title to view ACE's credit
recommendation. Be sure to check the dates offered to verify the exam is current.
http://www2.acenet.edu/credit/?fuseaction=browse.getOrganizationDetail&FI
CE=300271. Accessed March 31, 2016.

[40] *Listening, reading, and grammar comprehension questions in multiple-choice
format* From Question 7 on the FAQ page: http://flats.byu.edu/faq.php.

[41] *Usually 12 to 16 lower-level* See the following two pages: http://flats.byu.edu/
flatsinfo.php and http://flats.byu.edu/faq.php (Questions 2, 3, and 4). Accessed
March 31, 2016.

[42] *ACE recommends: 6 or 9 lower-level* http://www2.acenet.edu/
credit/?fuseaction=browse.getOrganizationDetail&FICE=300172. Accessed March
31, 2016.

[43] **Up to 16 at COSC and TESU** Charter Oak State College: http://www.charteroak.edu/catalog/current/sources_credit/testing_programs.cfm.
Thomas Edison State University: http://www.tesu.edu/academics/catalog/NYU-Foreign-Language-Proficiency.cfm. Accessed March 31, 2016.

[44] **4 lower-level for each elementary exam and 3 lower-level for each intermediate exam at Ohio University** http://www.catalogs.ohio.edu/content.php?catoid=45&navoid=3074. Accessed March 31, 2016.

[45] **The cost of this course is set by the college.** "The tuition for LearningCounts is set by the college or university where you enroll in the course." https://learningcounts.com/portfolio-assessment/how-to-enroll.

[46] **what types of knowledge and experience are best suited to prior learning assessment.** The following link provides course titles, descriptions, and credit recommendations of courses that can be completed via LearningCounts portfolios: http://www.nationalccrs.org/content/portfolio-course-listings.

[47] **Each portfolio corresponds to one undergraduate college course,** https://learningcounts.com/portfolio-assessment/how-to-enroll.
the average number of credits earned through portfolios is nine. https://learningcounts.org/. Accessed March 30, 2016.

[48] **list of approved tests for reimbursement** http://www.benefits.va.gov/gibill/national_testing.asp. Accessed March 30, 2016.

[49] **the ACE College Credit for Military Service page** ACE College Credit for Military Service page: http://www.acenet.edu/higher-education/topics/Pages/College-Credit-for-Military-Service.aspx.

[50] **The Army, Coast Guard, Marine Corps, National Guard, and Navy use the Joint Services Transcript** The Joint Services Transcript System: https://jst.doded.mil/.

[51] **Air Force members will receive a transcript from the Community College of the Air Force.** http://www.au.af.mil/au/barnes/ccaf/transcripts.asp.

[52] **navigate to the "National Emergency Training Center (NFA)."** The direct link follows: http://www2.acenet.edu/credit/?fuseaction=browse.getOrganizationDetail&FICE=300536.

[53] **ACE recommendations and the course offerings are updated periodically** ACE's credit recommendations for Penn Foster courses: http://www2.acenet.edu/credit/?fuseaction=browse.getOrganizationDetail&FICE=191627.

[54] **three credits for completing the course and no credit for your experiences** The Prior Learning Assessment page on Thomas Edison State University's website offers details of the program as well as a FAQ section. http://www.tesu.edu/degree-completion/PLA.cfm.

[55] **current portfolio requirements and process** TESU'S Prior Learning Assessment Course Description Database can help you discover subjects in which you may have learning worth college credit: http://www2.tesu.edu/plasearch.php.

[56] **portfolio processes comparable to TESU** Other colleges offering portfolio assessment are listed in a public spreadsheet maintained by Saylor.org (see link near the bottom of page): http://www.saylor.org/credit/.

[57] **a free personalized degree** https://www.straighterline.com/get-your-degree-plan/.

[58] **TECEP exams can also be transferred** Charter Oak State College: The following webpage contains a link to the "Master List of Credit Value of Specific Exams," which includes TECEP exams: http://www.charteroak.edu/exams/list-of-exams.cfm. Excelsior College: Though EC's website does not specifically mention TECEP exam credit, this credit falls under the policies for accredited college coursework: http://www.excelsior.edu/transfer-more-credits. See this DegreeForum.net post regarding transferring TECEP exam credit to other colleges: http://www.degreeforum.net/general-education-testing-discussion/22264-teceps-do-not-need-ace-nccrs.html.

[59] **per-credit cost varies** I calculated this per-credit cost to correspond with the CLEP per-credit cost in endnote 22. As in that estimate, I assumed that 50% of the degree from TESU was earned using CLEP or a similarly-priced credit-by-exam test. For the other 50%, instead of assuming that all 60 credits were from online courses, I assumed that 42 credits were from online TESU courses and 18 credits were from TECEP exams. In terms of the Comprehensive Tuition Plan, TECEP exams are not treated differently from online courses, so the per-credit TECEP cost would be identical to the per-credit CLEP cost in this scenario.
If you take fewer online courses from TESU and more TECEP exams, you may not need the benefits of the Comprehensive Tuition Plan (a year's worth of enrollment and up to 36 credits covered), and you may save money by choosing the Per Credit Tuition Plan. (TESU has a handy chart comparing the tuition plans here: http://www.tesu.edu/tuition/selecting-the-right-plan.cfm.) The only caveat to this plan is that there are academic residency requirements *if* you plan to earn a degree from TESU. However, don't be fooled by the word *residency* and think you will need to go on campus to meet these requirements because that is not the case. Actually, the requirements are as follows: "Students who select the Per Credit Tuition Plan (excluding those who enroll under a military or corporate plan) with the intention of earning an associates or bachelor's degree from Thomas Edison State University must complete 16 credits via Thomas Edison State University Online (OL), Guided Study (GS) or e-Pack® (EP) courses. This requirement may be waived by paying the Residency Waiver fee." The Residency Waiver Fee is $2,000. The Per Credit Plan also requires you to pay $300 for the one-credit cornerstone course. Per http://www.tesu.edu/tuition/Per-Credit.cfm and http://www.tesu.edu/tuition/Fees.cfm. To continue with my per-credit cost example, say you earned your first 60 credits through CLEP, but for the second 60 credits, you earned 18 credits from online TESU courses and 42 credits from TECEP exams. Just like the CLEP per-credit cost, I assume the second 60 credits are earned over a two-year period.
Per-Credit Tuition Plan: $11,276 for 60 credits over 2 years plus $1,760 for 16 CLEP

tests equals $13,036. Per-credit cost: $109.

TECEP exams are eligible for reimbursement under the GI Bill. See the following webpage: http://www.benefits.va.gov/gibill/national_testing.asp. Accessed April 1, 2016.

[60] **following the guidelines on TESU's website** http://www.tesu.edu/degree-completion/Testing-Arrangements.cfm.

[61] **view any of the outlines** List of available TECEP exams: http://www2.tesu.edu/listalltecep.php.

[62] **One way to locate these courses** The direct link to these courses is: https://teex.org/Pages/Program.aspx?catID=607.

[63] **earn a total of six college credits** To put your completed courses on a transcript, first transfer your TEEX courses to ACE, following the steps outlined here: https://www2.acenet.edu/credit/?fuseaction=transcripts.main. You will then be able to send your ACE transcript to the college of your choice. ACE charges $40 to send this transcript to one college and $15 for each college thereafter.

[64] **the exams have been recommended for credit by the ACE** http://www.excelsior.edu/who-accepts-uexcel-credits and http://www2.acenet.edu/credit/?fuseaction=browse.getOrganizationDetail&FICE=300321.

[65] **lower-level undergraduate UExcel exam is typically $95** According to page 2 of the Undergraduate Fee Schedule PDF available here: http://www.excelsior.edu/costs-and-financing/docs, the cost of UExcel exams "ranges from $40 to $460, depending upon their length and the credit that can be earned." The cost for a specific UExcel exam can be found by selecting an exam from this page: http://www.excelsior.edu/exams/choose-your-exam.
UExcel exam practice tests are generally between $18 and $75 apiece.
Veterans can apply for reimbursement for UExcel exams here: http://www.benefits.va.gov/gibill/national_testing.asp. Accessed March 24, 2016.

[66] **the definition of procrastinate** procrastinate Dictionary.com, *Collins English Dictionary - Complete & Unabridged 10th Edition*, HarperCollins Publishers. http://dictionary.reference.com/browse/procrastinate.

[67] **another definition of procrastination** procrastination. Dictionary.com, *Dictionary.com Unabridged,* Random House, Inc. http://dictionary.reference.com/browse/procrastination.

[68] **"A little sleep, a little slumber"** Proverbs 24:33-34, The Holy Bible, English Standard Version Copyright © 2001 by Crossway Bibles, a division of Good News Publishers.

[69] **structured or productive procrastination** John Tierney, "This Was Supposed to Be My Column for New Year's Day," *The New York Times*, January 14, 2013. http://www.nytimes.com/2013/01/15/science/positive-procrastination-not-an-oxymoron.html.

[70] **study periods punctuated with short breaks** In one study, a group of 84 participants were given a task to complete over 50 minutes. Those who had two small breaks remained focused throughout the experiment and, unlike the control group, experienced no drop in performance.

Atsunori Ariga and Alejandro Lleras, "Brief and rare mental 'breaks' keep you focused: Deactivation and reactivation of task goals preempt vigilance decrements," *Cognition* (2011), DOI: 10.1016/j.cognition.2010.12.007, http://news.illinois.edu/WebsandThumbs/Lleras,Alejandro/Lleras_sdarticle-17.pdf.

Rick Nauert, "Taking Breaks Found to Improve Attention," *Psych Central*, February 9, 2011. http://psychcentral.com/news/2011/02/09/taking-breaks-found-to-improve-attention/23329.html.

In another study, participants were tested for improved memory recall when memory encoding tasks were followed by a period of rest. This rest appears to give the brain time to process what was just learned, leading to higher recall.

Arielle Tambini, Nicholas Ketz, and Lila Davachi, "Enhanced Brain Correlations during Rest Are Related to Memory for Recent Experiences," *Neuron*, 65(2) pp. 280-290, January 28, 2010. DOI: 10.1016/j.neuron.2010.01.001, http://www.sciencedirect.com/science/article/pii/S0896627310000061.

Catherine Paddock, "Wakeful Resting Linked To Improved Memory," *Medical News Today*, February 1, 2010.
http://www.medicalnewstoday.com/articles/177782.php.

[71] **a common schedule known as the Pomodoro technique** http://pomodorotechnique.com/.

[72] **work and then have a day of rest** "Six days you shall work, but on the seventh day you shall rest; in plowing time and in harvest you shall rest." Exodus 34:21. Scripture taken from the New King James Version®. Copyright © 1982 by Thomas Nelson. Used by permission. All rights reserved.

[73] **refuge, protection, and purpose in life** "I will say of the LORD, 'He is my refuge and my fortress; my God, in Him I will trust.' Surely He shall deliver you from the snare of the fowler and from the perilous pestilence. He shall cover you with His feathers, and under His wings you shall take refuge; His truth shall be your shield and buckler. You shall not be afraid of the terror by night, nor of the arrow that flies by day, nor of the pestilence that walks in darkness, nor of the destruction that lays waste at noonday." Psalm 91:2-6. Scripture taken from the New King James Version®. Copyright © 1982 by Thomas Nelson. Used by permission. All rights reserved.

We were created by God for His glory and to give Him glory:
"For by him all things were created, in heaven and on earth, visible and invisible, whether thrones or dominions or rulers or authorities—all things were created through him and for him." Colossians 1:16 (ESV) The Holy Bible, English Standard Version Copyright © 2001 by Crossway Bibles, a division of Good News Publishers.

"Bring my sons from afar and my daughters from the end of the earth, everyone who is called by my name, *whom I created for my glory*, whom I formed and made." Isaiah 43:7 (ESV, emphasis added.)

"So, whether you eat or drink or whatever you do, do all to the glory of God." 1 Corinthians 10:31 (ESV)

[74] **the secretary of education to put forth a list of accrediting agencies** "History of Accreditation," Accrediting Council for Independent Colleges and Schools, http://www.acics.org/accreditation/content.aspx?id=2258.

[75] **The ED does not accredit educational institutions and/or programs** http://www2.ed.gov/admins/finaid/accred/accreditation.html.

[76] **The Council for Higher Education Accreditation (CHEA)** CHEA At-A-Glance (PDF) available here under the "About CHEA" heading: http://www.chea.org/.

[77] **27 of these accreditors were both ED- and CHEA-recognized** http://www.chea.org/pdf/CHEA_USDE_AllAccred.pdf.

[78] **"an ongoing status that must be reaffirmed periodically."** Accreditation as defined by the Northwest Commission on Colleges and Universities. http://www.nwccu.org/Process/Accreditation/Accreditation.htm.

[79] **credits you can use later in life** Jennifer Cook-DeRosa, *Homeschooling for College Credit* (2012), 55-58.

[80] **Database of Accredited Postsecondary Institutions and Programs** http://ope.ed.gov/accreditation/.

[81] **not always laid out clearly by regionally accredited colleges** "TRANSFER STUDENTS: Postsecondary Institutions Could Promote More Consistent Consideration of Coursework by Not Basing Determinations on Accreditation," United States Government Accountability Office (October 2005), 9, http://www.gao.gov/new.items/d0622.pdf.

[82] **portable credits** "Smart students should focus their attention on the quality of teaching, the portability of their credits, and the value a degree or other credential will provide them in the job market." Jeffrey J. Selingo, *College (Un)Bound* (Boston: Houghton Mifflin Harcourt, 2013), XVIII.

[83] **"where they will learn the most."** Derek Bok, *Universities in the Marketplace* (Princeton: Princeton University Press, 2003), 161.

[84] **"no bottom-line evaluation method exists"** Jeffrey J. Selingo, *College (Un)Bound* (Boston: Houghton Mifflin Harcourt, 2013), 24-25.

[85] **classes like these may not use technology to its full potential** Ibid., 203.

[86] **"cost per degree conferred."** William G. Bowen, *Higher Education in the Digital Age* (Princeton: Princeton University Press, 2013), 33, note 34.

[87] **between $550 and $1,100 (plus approximately $400-$600 for the cost of study materials)** To estimate the cost of study materials, I added nine months of InstantCert ($180), $40 per test for books ($200-$400), and $20 for the *CLEP Official Study Guide*.

[88] *the average cost of attending college* Trends in Higher Education, "Average Published Undergraduate Charges by Sector, 2014-15," The College Board, http://trends.collegeboard.org/college-pricing/figures-tables/average-published-undergraduate-charges-sector-2015-16.

not including books and supplies, https://bigfuture.collegeboard.org/pay-for-college/college-costs/quick-guide-college-costs. Accessed March 28, 2016.

[89] *be 16 years or older and possess nine or more acceptable college-level credits* http://www.charteroak.edu/prospective/apply/index.cfm.

[90] *a three-credit cornerstone course and a three-credit capstone course* Note: You must take the cornerstone course during the first term you are enrolled. Cornerstone and capstone course information: http://www.charteroak.edu/prospective/programs/degreesteps.cfm and http://www.charteroak.edu/prospective/admissions/faq.cfm#13.

[91] *a limit of 87 credits that can be transferred from community colleges* http://www.charteroak.edu/community-college/.

[92] *Tuition for online courses is calculated per credit* http://www.charteroak.edu/prospective/tuition/.

[93] *eligible for admission* See "Special Student Policy - High School Equivalency" for details: http://www.excelsior.edu/special-student-policy-high-school-equivalency.

[94] *three-credit information literacy course* https://info.excelsior.edu/student-policies/information-literacy-requirement/.

[95] *policy on community college credit* http://www.excelsior.edu/web/partners/community-colleges.

[96] *the per-credit tuition rate* http://www.excelsior.edu/costs-and-financing/undergraduate. Accessed March 28, 2016.

[97] *may request special consideration* http://www.tesu.edu/admissions/undergrad-admissions.cfm.

[98] *TESU accepts 80 community college credits and 120 from a regionally accredited four-year institution.* http://www.tesu.edu/admissions/Transfer-Credit.cfm.

[99] *tuition per credit varies* http://www.tesu.edu/tuition/tuition-fees.cfm. Accessed March 25, 2016.

[100] *Bachelor of Science in Business Administration* http://www.charteroak.edu/catalog/current/prog_study_degree_requirements/ and https://www.charteroak.edu/business-administration/. Accessed March 25, 2016.

[101] **Bachelor of Science in Business (Marketing)** http://www.excelsior.edu/programs/ business/bachelor-degrees. (At the time of printing, you can view the credit requirements in chart form by following these steps: select the marketing degree concentration, scroll to the bottom of the page, and click to expand the "Excelsior College BS in Business Degree Credit Requirements." You will then see a link to view the credit requirements in chart form.) Accessed March 25, 2016.

[102] **Bachelor of Science in Business Administration degree in Marketing** http://www. tesu.edu/business/bsba/Marketing.cfm. Accessed March 25, 2016.

[103] **86.5% offer online courses** I. Elaine Allen and Jeff Seaman, "Changing Course: Ten Years of Tracking Online Education in the United States," Babson Survey Research Group (2013), pp. 20, 32 and 37: http://onlinelearningsurvey.com/reports/ changingcourse.pdf.

[104] **Admission requirements** http://www.kaplanuniversity.edu/admissions/general-admissions-requirements.aspx.

[105] **prior learning credits** Types of credit Kaplan University may accept for credit: http:// catalog.kaplanuniversity.edu/Types_of_Credit.aspx.
for up to 75% of their degree http://www.kaplanuniversity.edu/paying-school/tuition-reduction.aspx. (See endnote 5.)

[106] **per-credit tuition for undergraduate online programs** http://www.kaplanuniversity. edu/paying-school/tuition-reduction.aspx. Accessed March 25, 2016.

[107] **One notable course** https://opencollege.kaplan.com/opencollege/LRC100/.

[108] **Admission requirements** http://www.liberty.edu/undergrad/index.cfm?PID=22981.

[109] **a dual enrollment program** The Edge admission requirements: http://www.liberty. edu/onlineacademy/dual-enrollment-admissions/.
About The Edge program: http://www.liberty.edu/onlineacademy/dual-enrollment/. Accessed March 24, 2016.

[110] **The per-credit cost for undergraduate online courses** http://www.liberty.edu/ financeadmin/financialaid/index.cfm?PID=22517. Accessed March 24, 2016.

[111] **up to 30 credits (31 for nursing students who hold their RN license)** http://www. liberty.edu/online/index.cfm?PID=14341 (see disclaimer at bottom of page) and http:// www.liberty.edu/online/index.cfm?PID=21814.

[112] **25 percent of the total degree** Academic catalog "Academic Information and Policies - Online Program" (see "Graduation Requirements" near the bottom of the webpage): https://www.liberty.edu/index.cfm?PID=31137.

[113] **free Unofficial Transfer Consultation** http://www.liberty.edu/online/index. cfm?PID=14342.

[114] **112 campus locations** http://www.phoenix.edu/campus-locations.html. Accessed March 24, 2016.

[115] **To apply, you must have** http://www.phoenix.edu/admissions/admission_requirements.html.

[116] **30 credits from national testing programs** http://www.phoenix.edu/tuition_and_financial_options/policies/credit_transfer_policy.html.

54 community college credits may transfer. http://www.phoenix.edu/alliance/communitycollege.html.

[117] **$410 per credit for 100/200-level courses** The only way I found to view tuition rates on University of Phoenix's website was to use the tuition and fees calculator here: http://www.phoenix.edu/tuition_and_financial_options/tuition_and_fees.html. Accessed March 24, 2016.

[118] **over 100 colleges and universities.** CollegePlus homepage: https://collegeplus.org/.

[119] **the degree outline page for the history degree** http://www.tesu.edu/heavin/ba/History.cfm. Accessed March 24, 2016.

[120] **These plans, especially those by DegreeForum.net user sanantone,** Sanantone's profile on DegreeForum.net: http://www.degreeforum.net/members/sanantone.html. Sanantone's BA in History on Degree Forum Wiki: http://degreeforum.wikia.com/wiki/Sanantone%27s_BA_in_History.
See the following page for other TESU degree plans: http://degreeforum.wikia.com/wiki/TESU_Degree_Plans. Accessed March 24, 2016.

[121] **information regarding the assessment-based degree** You can find the credit requirements for the assessment-based degrees on the following webpage: http://www.excelsior.edu/assessment_based_degree. You can earn a Bachelor of Arts in Liberal Studies or a Bachelor of Science in General Business.

[122] **68.4 percent of high school students attending college directly after graduation** Digest of Education Statistics (2015), "Table 302.10. Recent high school completers and their enrollment in 2-year and 4-year colleges, by sex: 1960 through 2014," U.S. Department of Education, Institute of Education Sciences, National Center for Education Statistics, accessed March 24, 2016. http://nces.ed.gov/programs/digest/d15/tables/dt15_302.10.asp.

[123] **"enjoy the benefits of a full collegiate experience"** Richard Arum and Josipa Roksa, *Academically Adrift* (Chicago: The University of Chicago Press, 2011), 124.

[124] **"social activities and interpersonal relationships as the main context for learning."** Rebekah Nathan, *My Freshman Year: What a Professor Learned by Becoming a Student* (New York: Penguin Books, 2006), 101. Rebekah Nathan is a pseudonym. As cited

in Richard Arum and Josipa Roksa, *Academically Adrift* (Chicago: The University of Chicago Press, 2011), 69.

[125] **The most significant college connections** Rebekah Nathan, *My Freshman Year: What a Professor Learned by Becoming a Student* (New York: Penguin Books, 2006), 56-58.

[126] **"collegiate culture [that] emphasizes sociability and encourages students to have fun"** Richard Arum and Josipa Roksa, *Academically Adrift* (Chicago: The University of Chicago Press, 2011), 120.

[127] **the idea of separating the teaching and credentialing** Salman Khan, *The One World Schoolhouse* (New York: Twelve, 2012), 229-232.

[128] **to better themselves and prepare for valuable credentials** Ibid., 232.

[129] **"the schoolroom, rather than being an artificial cloister"** Ibid., 194.

[130] **cannot continue learning** Ibid., 83-85 and 143-144.

[131] **answers to the questions of tomorrow** Jeffrey J. Selingo, *College (Un)Bound* (Boston: Houghton Mifflin Harcourt, 2013), 149.

[132] **perhaps only 20 percent of students would succeed** Salman Khan, *The One World Schoolhouse* (New York: Twelve, 2012), 253.
learning in a self-directed manner Ibid., 249.

[133] **"almost everyone will be motivated"** Ibid., 253.

[134] **"Students do not view debt exclusively as an investment,"** Steven Brint and Mathew Baron Rotondi, "Student Debt, the College Experience, and Transitions to Adulthood" (paper presented at the annual meeting for the American Sociological Association, Boston, July 31-August 4, 2008), 5.

[135] **an effect on buying a home and a car.** Ibid., 22-24.

[136] **less likely to purchase a home** Phyllis Korkki, "The Ripple Effects of Rising Student Debt" *The New York Times*, May 24, 2014, http://www.nytimes.com/2014/05/25/business/the-ripple-effects-of-rising-student-debt.html.

[137] **was seven times greater** This is a fascinating analysis of student debt's effect on economic conditions of young Americans. Richard Fry, "Young Adults, Student Debt and Economic Well-Being" Pew Research Center, Washington, D.C., May 14, 2014, http://www.pewsocialtrends.org/2014/05/14/young-adults-student-debt-and-economic-well-being/.

[138] **individuals' physical well-being and sense of purpose.** Allie Bidwell, "Student Debt Hurts More Than Your Wallet" *U.S. News & World Report*, August 7, 2014, http://www.usnews.com/news/articles/2014/08/07/having-high-levels-of-student-loan-debt-can-hurt-your-health-too.

[139] *Debt negatively affected all five.* Allie Bidwell, "Gallup: College Type Has Little to Do With Success" *U.S. News & World Report*, May 6, 2014, http://www.usnews.com/news/articles/2014/05/06/gallup-purdue-index-measures-the-magic-equation-to-student-success.

[140] *an accredited institution.* http://www2.ed.gov/admins/finaid/accred/accreditation_pg9.html. Accessed March 24, 2016.

[141] *B-Level scores for CLEP tests,* http://clep.collegeboard.org/develop/ace-credit.

[142] *TESU's CLEP page in the Undergraduate University Catalog* See page 100 in the Undergraduate University Catalog available here: http://www.tesu.edu/academics/catalog/index.cfm. Accessed March 24, 2016.

[143] *CLEP and DSST Overlap List* http://www.free-clep-prep.com/CLEP-and-DSST-Overlap-List.html.
CLEP Difficulty List http://www.free-clep-prep.com/clep-difficulty-list.html.

[144] *offered directly from TESU* http://www.tesu.edu/degree-completion/PLA-100-and-PLA-200.cfm.

[145] *the open version of these two courses* http://www.tesu.edu/academics/cal/Open-Education.cfm.
Completion of the open courses does allow you to submit portfolios to TESU. See Milestone 2 on this page: https://learn.saylor.org/course/view.php?id=375&sectionid=7224.

[146] *the one available from Kaplan* https://opencollege.kaplan.com/opencollege/LRC100/. March 24, 2016.

[147] *Dictionary.com says* accreditation. Dictionary.com, *Dictionary.com Unabridged*, Random House, Inc. http://www.dictionary.com/browse/accredit.

[148] *Charter Oak State College* http://www.charteroak.edu/community-college/. Accessed March 24, 2016.

[149] *Excelsior College* http://www.excelsior.edu/web/partners/community-colleges. Accessed March 24, 2016.

[150] *Thomas Edison State University* http://www.tesu.edu/admissions/Transfer-Credit.cfm. Accessed March 24, 2016.

[151] *University of Phoenix* http://www.phoenix.edu/alliance/communitycollege.html. Accessed March 24, 2016.

[152] *30 from national testing programs* http://www.phoenix.edu/tuition_and_financial_options/policies/credit_transfer_policy.html. Accessed March 24, 2016.

[153] ***three-credit cornerstone course and three-credit capstone course.*** http://www. charteroak.edu/prospective/new/advantages.cfm. Accessed March 24, 2016.

[154] ***three-credit capstone course.*** See Excelsior's bachelor's degree course requirements; the following link to the bachelor's degree in history credit requirements page is an example: http://www.excelsior.edu/programs/liberal-arts/history-bachelor-degree. Accessed March 24, 2016.

[155] ***one-credit cornerstone course*** http://www.tesu.edu/tuition/Per-Credit.cfm. ***three-credit capstone course*** See Thomas Edison State University's course requirements listed for each bachelor's degree. The following link to the Bachelor of Science in Business Administration course outlines shows the lack of a capstone requirement: http://www.tesu.edu/business/bsba/. Accessed March 24, 2016.

[156] ***graduating in a state of well-being.*** As quoted in *U.S. News & World Report*, a 2014 Gallup-Purdue study found that students' overall success and well-being were not tied to the selectivity of college they attended, the majors they chose, or even if they went to an Ivy League school. Rather, factors that had some influence were the school's size and whether the school was nonprofit or for-profit. (Larger or nonprofit schools improved the likelihood of students thriving.) Factors that doubled the odds of workplace engagement and well-being included being emotionally supported during college ("those who had at least one professor who made them excited about learning, professors who cared about them as a person and a mentor who encouraged them") and experiencing "'experiential and deep learning' – through a long-term project, an internship or a job and extreme involvement in extracurricular activities." Allie Bidwell, "Gallup: College Type Has Little to Do With Success," *U.S. News & World Report*, May 6, 2014, http://www.usnews.com/news/articles/2014/05/06/gallup-purdue-index-measures-the-magic-equation-to-student-success.

[157] ***"29 percent reported that they had never discussed ideas"*** National Survey of Student Engagement, *Experiences That Matter: Enhancing Student Learning and Success* (Bloomington, IN: Center for Postsecondary Research, Indiana University Bloomington, 2007), 46. As cited in Richard Arum and Josipa Roksa, *Academically Adrift* (Chicago: The University of Chicago Press, 2011), 95-96.

[158] ***approximately once per month.*** Richard Arum and Josipa Roksa, *Academically Adrift* (Chicago: The University of Chicago Press, 2011), 64.

[159] ***improvement on the CLA test became smaller.*** Ibid., 100.

[160] ***studied alone less than nine hours per week.*** Ibid., 115-116.

[161] ***students spending time in fraternities and sororities*** Ibid., 103.

[162] ***Facebook released a compilation of findings*** *From Classmates to Soulmates*, data analysis by Sofus Attila Macskassy and Lada Adamic, researchers on the Facebook Data Science Team, October 7, 2013. https://www.facebook.com/notes/facebook-data-science/from-classmates-to-soulmates/10151779448773859.

[163] **42 percent had met their spouse or partner at college.** Richard Arum, Esther Cho, Jeannie Kim, and Josipa Roksa, *Documenting Uncertain Times: Post-graduate Transitions of the Academically Adrift Cohort* (New York: Social Science Research Council, 2012), 13, 24.

[164] **The scoring range for this test Per page** 1 of the Technical Data Sheet PDF, available here: http://getcollegecredit.com/exam_fact_sheets.

INDEX

official website: hhtp://clep.
  collegeboard.org, 38, 42
owned by Educational Testing Service
  (ETS), 50
and pretests, 42–43
and proctoring, 164
readiness to take, 44–45, 170
scores kept on file for 20 years, 19, 53
sending scores to college before
  enrolled, 167
Specific Exam Feedback section of
  DegreeForum.net offering threads
  on CLEP tests, 36
step-by-step guide
  choosing a test, 31–32
  finding a test center, 30–31
  your college's policy
    concerning, 30–31
study resources for, 34–41, 74
  using college textbooks to
    study for, 170
taking CLEP tests while in high school,
  9, 29, 32, 51
testing day, 45–46
test scores compared to college letter
  grades, 165–66
time spent preparing for the test, 170
using testing as way to meet others,
  148–49
verifying your schedule with the
  testing center, 45
what to do if a college doesn't accept
  CLEP tests, 114–15
what to expect from CLEP test credits,
  165
who will benefit from taking CLEP
  tests, 30
CollegePlus, 24–25, 27, 97
helping create a custom degree plan,
  129, 143
colleges and universities
benefits of not exclusive to the
  campus, 149–50
choosing the degree and the college,
  109–127, 177–80
college accreditation in the US,
  101–108
  finding accreditation status of
    a school, 107, 108
college campus experience, 9–10
college's website as useful tool,
  92–93, 98
companies recommending number
  of credits a course is worth, 12,

61–62, 68, 69, 70, 78
costs of attending, 1, 6–7, 18, 23,
  46–47, 211n1, 214n20
  average room and board, 18,
    212n7
  compared to taking CLEP
    tests, 46–47
  cost of earning a degree,
    113–14
  increasing costs of, 6, 212n4
  for sending test scores to
    college, 3, 17
creating customized college goals, 10
difference between applying and
  enrolling, 176
graduating in a state of well-being,
  179, 227n156
high school students going directly to
  after graduation, 147
learning, socialization, and
  credentialing all goals for going
  to college, 14, 145–48, 153–54,
  158, 160
parents and students expectations
  for, 147
preparing for life after college, 156–60
reasons for going to, 5–6
sending CLEP and DSST test scores
  to, 52
ways college can help off-campus
  students, 93–95
Collegiate Learning Assessment (CLA), 182
Comex, 34–35
community college course credits, 63–64. See
  also associate degrees
  transfer of at COSC, 64
  transfer of at EC, 64
  transfer of at TESU, 64, 117, 222n98
Community College of the Air Force (CCAF),
  72
competency based exams (CBE), 139
CompTIA A+ (test measuring computer
  technician competency), 19–20, 93, 174,
  212n9. See also Information Systems,
  resources used for CLEP test
connections, making, 145–56
Cook-DeRosa, Jennifer, 23, 106–107
  on Pell Grants, 212n10
cornerstone courses, 222n90
  at COSC, 116, 179
  at TESU, 117, 122, 179
COSC. See Charter Oak State College (COSC)
costs
  affect of college debt, 163

CPSIA information can be obtained
at www.ICGtesting.com
Printed in the USA
FSOW02n1819030916
24507FS

9 780997 308006